# LITANIES AND OTHER PRAYERS

This volume follows the new Revised Common Lectionary. Where necessary, the materials of the first edition of *Litanies and Other Prayers* have been altered or replaced to accommodate the new readings. The three-year lectionary cycle remains unchanged: Year A begins in Advent 1992 and 1995; Year B in Advent 1993 and 1996; Year C in Advent 1994 and 1997.

# Litanies
## and
# Other
# Prayers

## FOR THE REVISED
## COMMON LECTIONARY

## YEAR C

*Phyllis Cole*
*Everett Tilson*

ABINGDON PRESS
Nashville

LITANIES AND OTHER PRAYERS FOR
THE REVISED COMMON LECTIONARY
Year C

*This book is printed on recycled, acid-free paper.*

**Library of Congress Cataloging-in-Publication Data**

Cole, Phyllis, 1962–
    Litanies and other prayers for the Revised common lectionary.
    Year C/Phyllis Cole, Everett Tilson.
        p.    cm.
    Includes index.
    ISBN 0-687-22122-6 (pbk.: alk. paper)
    1. Church year—Prayer-books and devotions—English.    2. Litanies.
3. Pastoral prayers.    4. Common lectionary (1992)    I. Tilson,
Everett.    II. Title.
BV30.C594    1994
264'.13—dc20                                                                93-42153
                                                                                    CIP

MANUFACTURED IN THE UNITED STATES OF AMERICA

# Contents

# Introduction

This project (of which this is the third volume) is serendipity's child. The two of us were asked to write the prayers and litanies for the inauguration of the new president of the Methodist Theological School. To begin, we launched a painstaking search for models. Not greatly encouraged by what we found, we decided to create our own, interweaving the themes and images of the biblical passages selected for the occasion. This dialogue with Scripture, undertaken on behalf of a seminary community at worship, soon turned frustration into excitement. Biblical and contemporary images and ideas came together in meaningful and expressive fashion. Later we were pleased by the response to our efforts. Yet we were even more gratified by the challenge and insight we experienced in the writing. We felt that we had found a pattern by which to compose liturgical materials for Sunday services, as well as special occasions.

While one of us is ordained and the other not, our experience in the worship of the church has been more alike than different. Both of us first worshiped in small-town or rural churches. There the lections for any given Sunday were those chosen by the minister, usually for reasons known to the minister alone. Few of these ministers consciously tried to establish a thematic unity between the scripture lessons and other elements of the service. While this failure was not unforgivable, our experience of worship would have been enriched if such unity had been achieved.

From the first century, the Scriptures have played a unifying role in Christian worship, which follows the pattern of Jewish tradition. The Protestant emphasis on the primacy of the Word heightened this focus, as illustrated by the hymns of Isaac Watts and Charles Wesley. Watts' hymns were often little more than a deliberate rendering of the psalms into the contemporary English idiom. Wesley's hymns, reflecting a more comprehensive and evangelical use of the Bible, were no less inspired by the Scriptures.

In the course of time, however, the influence of the Bible on hymns and other elements of the service faded. Eventually the doctrine of the priesthood of all believers yielded a growing enthusiasm for lay participation in worship. This development was accompanied by a decreasing dependence on Scripture for liturgical expression. The liturgical imagination, shaped by tradition, became increasingly captive to the inspiration of the moment. The assumption survived that the sermon should be intimately connected to the Scriptures, but the unity between other elements of the service and the scripture readings suffered.

The ecumenical movement has prompted us to lament this loss, and it has led Protestantism to a rediscovery of the lectionary. This, in turn, has kindled a new awareness of the need for both the *conscious integration of all the elements of the service* and their *dynamic interaction with the Scriptures*. Many resources are available which suggest complementary lections, hymns, invocations, and benedictions, and in increasing numbers, these are based on the lectionary.

We regret that fuller lay participation in worship has contributed to the misuse—or nonuse—of the lectionary, but we would be the last to recommend *less* lay participation. The sanctity of the common life kept the movement behind the Protestant Reformation from becoming a backward movement. The common life enabled the Reformers to connect the past to the present, giving new shape to the future and also to Christian liturgy. What we seek now is not less but *deeper* lay participation—participation that is informed and enriched by symbolism born of the encounter between religious tradition and modern life.

The renewed emphasis on spiritual formation has encouraged such participation, but this development has been a mixed blessing. For some worshipers, it has had the unfortunate effect of turning the heart inward upon itself, rather than upward to God and outward to the neighbor. And, instead of bringing individuals closer together, it has sometimes set them apart, baptizing the notion that interest in one's soul rightfully may become one's sole interest.

Theoretically, use of the lectionary should prevent such distortion of the gospel, since its readings have been chosen *by* the community *for* the community. Ironically, though, this recovery of "spirituality" has led many churches to a preoccupation with worship, just as it has led many individuals to a preoccupation with personal piety. Rather than turning the church outward to the world, it sometimes has turned the church inward upon itself. When the reformation of liturgical life is not accompanied by the transformation of public life, spirituality becomes heresy. Authentic spirituality expresses itself not only in services of worship, but also in worshipful service. It may take root in the sanctuary, but it must bear fruit in the street. It may begin with individual reflection in church, but it will not end until it has produced corporate action in society.

In recent works on the lectionary, such social awareness has been most evident in the attention paid to inclusive language. They have especially addressed—and tried to redress—sexist language in the lections. Their recognition of the role language plays in reflecting and in shaping our beliefs and behavior has been critical for the church. And, fortunately, these efforts have persisted despite criticism from some church circles.

But sexism is not the only villain that divides the Christian community and the human family. Evil wears many other masks—racism, nationalism, classism, ageism, and handicappism, to mention only a few. To overcome these divisive forces, we can begin by reforming the words we use, but we must dig beneath those words to their underlying attitudes. Words that exclude and offend spring from hearts that fail to include and affirm. Their use testifies to something far more serious than a failure of language. It witnesses to the failure of faith.

Our faithful worship of the Lord as the God of all creation obliges us to cut the cloth of human concern on the pattern of divine love. And that obligation calls us to search for words whose use will break down the ugly walls that separate persons of different genders, ethnic groups, nationalities, income levels, ages, and physical abilities. It is not enough merely to

11

avoid language that degrades and abuses other human beings. We must, instead, seek to speak words that will embrace and honor them. Our language in worship must be as inclusive as that traditional invitation to communion which calls to the table all "ye that do truly and earnestly repent of your sins, and are in love and charity with your neighbors."

Christians often cite our Lord's summary of the Great Commandment in the Decalogue (Matthew 22:34-40) as the hallmark statement of Christian inclusiveness. Yet we sometimes fail to recognize that statement's Old Testament roots. Such neglect of the Old Testament has characterized much Christian practice in the use of the lectionary. Despite the inclusion of its readings in lectionaries through the ages, the Old Testament has long suffered from inadequate attention in Christian preaching and worship. This oversight might be understandable if the content of New Testament lections did not so heavily rely on Old Testament language and imagery, and if New Testament theology did not so essentially derive its categories and their import from those of the Old Testament. We must, therefore, make a conscious and constant effort to correct this imbalance. Our aim must not be simply to give the Old Testament *its* due. We must also hope to give the New Testament *its* due, by tracing its ideas and images to their source.

Experts in communication have long recognized the importance of clothing truth in appealing language. The current stress in biblical studies on the use of imagery can be traced to this recognition. But imagery, to be clarifying and persuasive, must not only be vivid; it also must be visual. The hearer must be able to see what the speaker says. For this to happen, speakers must put themselves in the position of hearers, just as hearers must be able to put themselves in the position of speakers. We shall consciously strive, therefore, for language that will enable the users of this volume to hear with their eyes.

This resource assumes an intimate connection not only between the Bible and worship, but also between worship and vocation. Indeed, worship may be conceived as a bridge between the Bible and vocation, with traffic moving in both directions. For just as we have drawn on the biblical witness to find appropriate images for the prayers in this volume, we have so elaborated them as to amplify the tasks to which God calls us in our world.

On this point, two objections will be raised. Some will object that we have been more specific than we should have been about the nature of these tasks. We would reply that the biblical writers articulate the divine call in quite concrete and very particular terms. Others will feel that we have been less specific than we should have been. We would respond that it would be most unbiblical of God to reveal more to worshipers through the written word than through the spoken word. To the degree that we achieve our goal for this project, direct communication will proceed from indirect communication. God will take our place as your partner in dialogue.

Our use of imagery in these prayers is not limited to that found in the assigned lections. Biblical images, like biblical themes, leap the boundaries of books and chapters or verses to engage one another in dialogue. This thoughtful play of imagination, so obviously at work in the writing of the Bible, has inspired us in our reading of the Bible. We offer this reminder so that you will not be surprised when we employ imagery from other passages of Scripture to illuminate our presentation of the lectionary themes.

We offer one final piece of advice for the effective use of this volume: Alter these prayers in any way that will make them more fully your own—by changing the language for addressing deity, by deleting or substituting paragraphs, by localizing the points of reference. While we are responsible for the form the prayers take in this book, you are responsible for the form they will take in your worship.

# LITANIES AND OTHER PRAYERS

*Abbreviations*

| | |
|---|---|
| *A* | All |
| *L* | Leader |
| *M* | Men |
| *P* | People |
| *W* | Women |

# Advent Season

---

*Lections:* Jeremiah 33:14-16; Psalm 25:1-10; I Thessalonians 3:9-13; Luke 21:25-36

*Call to Worship*
L: The day foretold is coming,
P: When our tired eyes will behold a fire, a blazing star in the eastern sky!
L: The one foretold is coming—
P: Whose light will shine through the deepest gloom: a manger's glow in the silent night!
L: The day is at hand!
P: World, keep watch!
L: The savior draws near!
P: Praise the Lord!

*Invocation.* O God of the Coming One, we lift up our eyes, we lift up our souls in expectation! We trust; we will not be afraid, for you have promised to send a shepherd to reveal your paths and a teacher to show your ways.

We are mindful of our cruelty, Lord, so be mindful of your mercy, and send your shepherd soon! We are mindful of our spitefulness, so be mindful of your steadfast love, and dispatch your teacher here! For as we look upon your faithful servant, we shall see your shining face; and as we gaze into your steady eyes, we shall behold the image that is our own.[1]

*Litany*
L: O world, watch! Do not sleep—
P: For the realm of God is near!
L: In the midst of the wilderness lay a garden,
P: And in the garden stood a tree.
L: In the spring her roots drank the tears of God;

---

1 Inspired by Genesis 1:26.

P:   In the summer her leaves basked in the light of God's face;
L:   In the autumn her leaves danced on the breath of God;
P:   In the winter her buds slept in the warmth of God's bosom.
L:   But the tree grew old, a tired stump: The tears, once sweet, seemed to grow bitter; the face, once bright, to fade away;
P:   The breath, once gentle, seemed to bluster with spite; the bosom, once soft, to harden with cold.
L:   But look! The wilderness shall all be changed—
P:   For the tired stump is sprouting again, and a righteous branch shoots forth![2]
L:   The spirit of the Lord has fallen upon it:
P:   The spirit of wisdom and understanding, the spirit of counsel and might!
L:   From rotten roots and lifeless stump,
P:   The branch of God stretches toward its blossom—
L:   O world, watch! Do not sleep!
P:   The realm of God is near![3]

*Prayer for One Voice.* O Anointer of prophets and Sender of saviors, receive our prayer! Long have the seas roared, and long have we cried out, but the sound of our cries has been drowned by crashing waves and screaming winds. Only the battered earth has cupped an ear to hearken to our lament. Long have the mountains quaked, and long have we moaned, but our moans have been buried beneath cracking rocks and splitting timbers. Only the trembling earth has reached out to grasp our hand.

The earth has been a witness to our suffering, Lord, and she has also been its victim. If our hearts have been weighed down with the cares of this life, hers has been crushed by the cares of our lives. We have laden her with our poverty of spirit and our profusion of things; our neglect of truth and our need for deceit; our desire for comfort and our disdain for change; our practice of bigotry and our patience with hypocrisy; our indulgence of

---

2   Inspired by Job 14:7-9.
3   Drawn from Isaiah 11:1-3*a*.

ourselves and our indifference to our neighbors. These crosses and many more we have forced the earth to bear.

But now the burden has become too great. Our battles have bent her shoulders. Our quarrels have broken her back. Her face is disfigured, her body scarred. She stumbles, and falls; she can carry us no farther. We kneel over her: Her pulse is weak, the rivers are running dry; her breathing is shallow, the breezes are blowing ill.

We call upon you, Lord! Still the waves and calm the winds! Silence the rocks and hush the timbers! This earth cannot save us; like her inhabitants, she must be saved.

Help her, O Lord, by helping us! Raise up a healer among us to restore the earth! Call a prophet to announce your reign! Send a savior to reveal your love! Choose a servant to render your justice! Anoint a messiah to redeem your world!

We are watching, Lord! In all times, in all places, we watch for a sign that your Coming One is drawing near. We keep the vigil for ourselves and for the earth, for we must know the time of our visitation. Only the Coming One can ease the load and make all burdens light. Only the Coming One can transform our poverty of spirit into an abundance of faithfulness; our profusion of things into a storehouse of goods to share; our neglect of the truth into a commitment to the gospel; our need for deceit into a disgust for corruption; our desire for comfort into a dislike of conformity. Only the Coming One can transform our disdain for change into a drive toward creativity; our practice of bigotry into an intolerance of prejudice; our patience with hypocrisy into an insistence on sincerity; our indulgence of ourselves into the chastening of our vanity; our indifference to our neighbors into the hastening of our charity.

A new earth is leaping in the womb, Lord; a new humanity is kicking beneath your hand. Won't you deliver your messiah? We wait. We wonder. We watch.

*Benediction.* The day is at hand; the savior draws near! Let us watch, and let our eyes be clear, lest the star appear and not be followed, lest the child be born and not be found.

# LITANIES AND OTHER PRAYERS

## Second Sunday of Advent

*Lections:* Baruch 5:1-9; Malachi 3:1-4 (alternate); Psalm 126; Philippians 1:3-11; Luke 3:1-6

### Call to Worship

L: The day foretold is coming,
P: When our deafened ears will hear a choir, a heavenly host proclaiming peace!
L: The one foretold is coming—
P: Whose cry will pierce the deepest gloom: a newborn's wail in the silent night!
L: The day is at hand!
P: World, listen!
L: The savior draws near!
P: Praise the Lord!

*Invocation.* O God of the Coming One, we hear the voice of your messenger crying in our wilderness, saying, "Prepare the way of the Lord!" We trust; we will not be afraid, for you have promised that every valley shall be filled; every mountain, brought low; the crooked, made straight; the rough, made smooth.

This promise peals across the land, that the wilderness shall become your kingdom, that all flesh shall live to see your salvation. The ringing swells, the day approaches: Listen to our laughter—we are throwing off all garments of sorrow! Hearken to our shouts of joy, and wrap your children in robes of glory!

### Litany

L: O world, listen! Do not sleep—
P: For the realm of God is near!
L: Arise, and turn your eyes to the east,
P: Where the nations are gathering with shouts of joy,
L: Singing songs as at harvest-time,
P: Swelling the air with praise!
L: The Lord of life has remembered them,
P: The God of heaven has blessed the earth;
L: Their lamentations have become celebrations;
P: Their death march, the holy dance!
L: At the sound of their singing, the mountains are leveled;

18

P: At the sound of their laughter, the valleys are filled.

L: At the sound of their clapping, the crooked is made straight;

P: At the sound of their tramping, the rough is made smooth.

L: A voice cries out in the wilderness:

P: Prepare the way of the Lord!

L: O world, listen! Do not sleep!

P: The realm of God is near!

*Prayer for One Voice.* O God, you hold creation close to your heart. As you have loved her into being, your heart has been deeply wounded by her pain and wonderfully mended by her joy. From beginning to end, from small to great, from low to high, from near to far, from first to last, you have cared for her, tending her needs, sustaining her growth, easing her suffering, increasing her pleasure.

Then, having been fashioned by your hands and inspired by your breath, creation has surrounded us—to tend *our* needs, sustain *our* growth, ease *our* suffering, and increase *our* pleasure. This you have intended from the beginning, for you hold us, like her, close to your heart. You have entrusted us to her care because you have looked upon her and declared her good; and, at the same time, you have entrusted her to *our* care, for while capable of doing good, we must learn how through time and toil.

So you mean us to be partners in the gospel, Lord—partners with you, with creation, with one another. You mean us to partake together of the grace, the mercy, the abundance of this world. But the partnership has been broken—not because you have failed to hold us up, not because creation has let us down, but because we have proved unequal to—or worse, unmindful of—the task.

It was all you have ever asked of us, Lord—right offerings and good fruits. But we have kept the best offerings and ripest fruits for ourselves, while you have waited and creation has wasted away. We have frantically hoarded while our world has been depleted. We have leisurely washed our hands while our world has been defiled. We have hastened to endless feasts while our world has been denied. We have reveled without a care while our world has been raped. We have not noticed nature's need, but ignored it; not sustained her growth, but stunted it; not eased her suffering, but sharpened it; not increased her pleasure, but diminished it.

O God, save us all from one another, and save your world from our sin! Hear our cry! Send a savior who is one of us, who can understand us, and show us the way! We hearken to your word, Lord; we await the sounds of your coming! Do not forget us; do not delay!

*Benediction.* The day is at hand; the savior draws near! Let us listen, and let our ears be sharp, lest the cry arise and go unheeded, lest the angel sing and go unheard.

### Third Sunday of Advent

*Lections:* Zephaniah 3:14-20; Isaiah 12:2-6; Philippians 4:4-13; Luke 3:7-18

*Call to Worship*
L: The day foretold is coming,
P: When our bitter mouths will drink new wine, God's cup raised high at the kingdom's table!
L: The one foretold is coming—
P: Whose bread will be broken in deepest gloom: a last supper shared on a silent night!
L: The day is at hand!
P: World, feast!
L: The savior draws near!
P: Praise the Lord!

*Invocation.* O God of the Coming One, we have come to draw water from your well. We trust; we will not be afraid, for you have promised that the taste of this water will not be bitter, like the tears of our eyes, but sweet, like the honey of flowers.

From your well we will receive our baptism; from its waters we will accept our healing. All flesh shall gather here together, and the one who is lame shall leap for joy; the one who is outcast shall be brought in with gladness.

O God, pour out your salvation upon us who thirst, and where once was shame there shall be only praise.

*Litany*

L: O world, thirst, and feel your hunger—
P: For the realm of God is near!
L: Blessed are you who thirst for righteousness,
P: For soon you shall be satisfied:
L: Like the deer that longs for flowing streams,[4]
P: And the desert that hopes for cooling rains,
L: Your soul shall finally drink of God,
P: The spring of living water.[5]
L: Blessed are you who hunger for goodness,
P: For soon you shall be satisfied:
L: Manna from heaven shall descend upon you,[6]
P: And all shall partake of the bread of life;[7]
L: The nations shall break the loaf together—
P: Falling down upon their knees.
L: O world, thirst, and feel your hunger!
P: The realm of God is near!

*Prayer for One Voice.* O Lord our God, where a rainbow bends in the midst of thunder, or a flower blooms in the midst of sand, you are there. Where a dream persists in the midst of conflict, or a protest arises in the midst of calm, you are there. Where a candle glows in the midst of winter, or a river thaws in the midst of spring, you are there. Where a cradle rocks in the midst of suffering, or a hand is held in the midst of pain, you are there. Where a prayer ascends in the midst of cursing, or passion flares in the midst of uncaring, you are there.

O God, you are in our midst. And because you are here, you tell us, "Do not fear; let not your hands grow weak." But we are not so easily comforted; we are not so quickly inspired. You surround us, but we cannot see your face, we cannot hear your voice, we cannot feel your embrace. How can we trust you? How can we have courage? How can our hands be strong?

We confess this, Lord: We would rather trust ourselves. We would rather venerate our past—our pride in family lines,

---

4  See Matthew 5:6; Psalm 42:12.
5  Inspired by Psalm 143:6; John 4:13; 7:38.
6  See Genesis 16.
7  Inspired by Luke 1:53; John 6:35.

honored traditions, historic institutions. We would rather glorify our future—our opportunity for posterity, prosperity, and popularity. When we implore, "What shall we do?" we do not ask one of your locust-eating, leather-girdled prophets,[8] who would summon us to the wilderness and demand that we change our ways! Instead, we ask the keepers of our law, the caretakers of our culture, and the custodians of our religion, for we know that their answers will be pleasing to the taste. Their answers shall become *our* answers, dripping like honey from our tongues but falling like vinegar on your ears.

O Lord, how merciful you are for not forsaking us! You send us messenger after messenger, only to be mocked, and word after word, only to be despised.[9] Now your greatest messenger is about to be born, a messenger who not only will speak and do your word, but embody it. Do you know what you do? We can smile at a baby, but shall we not scorn the man? We can shelter the child, like a hen gathering her chicks under her wings,[10] but shall we shelter the Christ, or hide in the upper room?

O God, you send this child into our midst to make your presence among us tangible, visible, touchable. But will the child make you understandable, *acceptable* to the stoners and killers of prophets, to us who so easily become afraid, whose weak hands so quickly seek to crucify? Can truth really walk safely among the deceitful; or justice, among the vengeful; or love, among the hateful; or grace, among the spiteful?

Help us to trust you, Lord. We cannot comprehend this thing that is about to happen, this baby who will be our savior. We have learned well how we can be custodians of law, guardians of culture, and champions of religion; we do not know how—or if—we can be disciples of such a one as this. Prepare us for the bearer of the gospel, O God, lest we receive the good news as *bad* news, and turn our backs.

Be with us, Lord, as you send him to us. The thunder rumbles: Lead us to the bending rainbow. The sands creep:

---

8 See Matthew 3:4.
9 See II Chronicles 36:15-16.
10 Inspired by Matthew 23:37.

22

Lead us to the blooming flower. The winter blows: Lead us to the glowing candle. The spring breaks: Lead us to the thawing river.

The suffering one comes: Lead us to the rocking cradle!

*Benediction.* The day is at hand; the savior draws near! Let us feast, and let our taste be keen, lest the cup be filled and left unpoured, lest the bread be baked and left unbroken.

## Fourth Sunday of Advent

*Lections:* Micah 5:2-5*a*; Psalm 80:1-7; Hebrews 10:5-10; Luke 1:39-55

*Call to Worship*
L:  The day foretold is coming,
P:  When our sleeping hearts will stir again, entrusting their hope to swaddling clothes!
L:  The one foretold is coming—
P:  Whose touch will dispel the deepest gloom: God's hand holding ours in the silent night!
L:  The day is at hand!
P:  World, *feel!*
L:  The savior draws near!
P:  Praise the Lord!

*Invocation.* O God of the Coming One, how we long for salvation, and how we tremble at its advent! Yet we trust; we will not be afraid, for you have promised that the child leaping in the world's womb will exceed our hopes and expel our fears.

The labor is beginning, Lord. Soon the earth shall be in the throes of birth. Let the Coming One come forth! And let us, the brothers and sisters of this Child of Peace, feel the glory of nativity!

*Litany*
L:  O world, *feel!* Do not sleep—
P:  For the realm of God is near!
L:  The warmth of God's face will shine upon you;

P: Its peace will fall on your warring spirits.[11]
L: The word of God's mouth will fall upon you;
P: Its wisdom will baptize your foolish lips.
L: The strength of God's arm will work within you:
P: Its power will spread through your tired hands.
L: The love of God's heart will rise up within you;
P: Its mercy will quiet your troubled souls.
L: The life in God's womb will throb within you;
P: Its pulse will renew your fainthearted dreams.
L: God is not far from each of us,[12]
P: Only waiting to be touched:
L: O world, *feel!* Do not sleep!
P: The realm of God is near!

*Prayer for One Voice.* O God, your light is rising in the east. Some say it is a star, announcing the birth of a new ruler. Others believe it is the sun, breaking the dawn of a new age. Whatever it may be, this glorious event is of your doing, for from the beginning your hand has hung the great lights in the heavens.

The light has not yet arrived; its time is not yet come, but we await its coming with fear and with joy.

Fear—that the pride you have promised *then* to scatter is but the arrogance within us. Fear—that the might you have promised *then* to humble is but the cruelty within us. Fear—that the wealth you have promised *then* to spurn is but the greediness within us. Fear—that this light shall reveal what we have concealed, and challenge what we need to change.

Yet our trembling is mixed with rejoicing. Joy—that scarred hearts might love again. Joy—that downcast eyes might look up again. Joy—that empty mouths might eat again. Joy—that idle hands might work again. Joy—that tired spirits might play again.

We are afraid, and we are joyful, because when this light finally breaks in the east, signaling a new ruler, or a new age, or both, this world will be seen in a new way. What *is* will begin to disappear into the realm of what *was*. What was hoped for will begin to appear in the sphere of what can be. Old ones will

---

11 See Numbers 6:25-26.
12 See Acts 17:27.

24

hear and be born again. Little ones will speak with the wisdom of sages. First will be last, and last, first. High will be low, and low, high. Every fettered slave will be released, and all will serve your cause in freedom. Every blinded eye will receive sight, and all will gaze upon your face with love.

O Lord, soon your light will hover above the place where Mary lies. As we approach her, remove the density of our fear and increase the intensity of our joy. Lay our hand upon her, ever so gently, that we might greet the tiny messenger, the child come to do your will when we would not, or could not. Run our hand across her sweating brow, ever so slowly, for you would have us be the salt of earth. Lift our hand to feel her throat, filled with groans at the pangs of birth, even as we have groaned in travail until now, awaiting our salvation.[13]

Place our hand in Mary's, Lord. Let us touch her, that we might ease her suffering, and let her spirit touch us, that we might confess, with the shepherds and the magi who will join us at her side, "The child comes, and so have we."

*Benediction.* The day is at hand; the Savior draws near! Let us touch, and let our touch be lingering, lest the unborn leap and go unnoticed, lest the newborn tremble and go unloved.

---

13 Inspired by Mark 9:50; Romans 8:22-23.

25

# Christmas Season

## Christmas Eve/Day

*Lections:* Isaiah 9:2-7; Psalm 96; Titus 2:11-14; Luke 2:1-20

*Call to Worship*
L: We who dwelled in shadows have seen a great light:
P: Glory from heaven embraces the earth, like a mother's arms around a newborn child,
L: Tucking the earth in folds of peace, like a baby wrapped in swaddling clothes,
P: Laying the earth in the cradle of truth, like a baby entrusted to a manger.
L: As the cry of a baby splits the air, uniting the songs of shepherds and angels,
P: Let us give thanks for the birth of a child, through whose young life salvation shines!

*Invocation.* O God, place your trumpets in our hands, and we will make a mighty sound! For unto the world a child is born; unto the world a savior is given. His hands will split the yoke of our burdens; his knee will snap the rod of our afflictions. He will establish peace upon the earth, breaking the bow and shattering the spear, casting the boots of each tramping warrior into the leaping flames.[14]

You have struck the spark, Lord. The refiner's fire is kindled in the darkness; an ember glows in the silent night. Unto the world a child is born; unto the world a savior is given. Place your trumpets in our hands, and we shall call the world to peace![15]

*Litany*
L: Ascribe to the Lord, O families of nations, the *honor* due God's name—

---

14 Inspired by Judges 7:15-16; Psalm 46:9-10.
15 Inspired by Malachi 3:2; Isaiah 27:13.

26

P: The honor of a scandalous love, a love that kept Joseph by Mary's side when she became great with child!

L: Ascribe to the Lord, O families of nations, the *majesty* due God's name—

P: The majesty of a lowly manger, a manger that cradled a tiny savior when no room was found in the inn!

L: Ascribe to the Lord, O families of nations, the *power* due God's name—

P: The power of a simple shepherd, a shepherd who first beheld the One whose name was announced by a heavenly choir!

L: Ascribe to the Lord, O families of nations, the *beauty* due God's name—

P: The beauty of two ordinary parents, the parents who watched the magi kneel and pondered these things in their wondering hearts!

A: Honor! Majesty! Power! Beauty! Ascribe to the Lord, O families of nations, the *glory* due God's name!

*Prayer for One Voice.* O God, we have waited long in the fields of night, keeping watch over the flocks, looking for signs of the morning. And what a sign you have given! The birth of a child! The birth of a savior! The birth of new life! Through your tender mercy, a new day has dawned, giving light to us who sit in darkness and dwell in the shadow of death, revealing the path of righteousness and guiding our feet into the way of peace.[16]

This child who has been born among us—he is the one with whom you will be well pleased.[17] And he has been born not among the mighty, but the lowly; not among the ruling, but the ruled; not among the rich, but the poor; not among the favored, but the outcast.

He is not the messiah we had expected from you, Lord. But there is the star dancing above the stall, and there is the angelic choir singing overhead: "Glory to God in the highest, and on earth, peace!" All creation celebrates the sign that has come to the nations, the salvation that has come to the peoples. The

16 See Luke 1:78-79.
17 See Luke 3:22.

night has been broken; how can we doubt? The dawn is here; how can we not view the world in a different light?

We have run from the fields to see this thing that has happened; we have seen with our eyes—help us to understand with our hearts! O God, help us to know the time of our visitation, so that when the child, become a man, draws near to the place of our habitation, his heart might not be broken; that, instead of weeping, he might rejoice, saying, "Now you have learned the things that make for peace!"[18]

*Benediction.* Somewhere in the night of our lives, a baby cries, and that cry is our hope. The grace of God has appeared for the salvation of our world. Glory to God in the highest, and on earth, peace!

## First Sunday After Christmas

*Lections:* I Samuel 2:18-20, 26; Psalm 148; Colossians 3:12-17; Luke 2:41-52

*Call to Worship*
L:  We who knelt in the stable—
P:  Let us come and kneel in the temple!
L:  Let our hearts give thanks, and our hands rejoice!
P:  Let our spirits sing, and our bodies dance!
L:  O children, enter the house of the Lord!
P:  Enter God's presence, and be reborn!

*Invocation.* O Spirit, rise up from the earth to be with us in this place; descend from the heavens to be with us in this time. We have gathered to worship you, for such is the beginning of wisdom. In worship, we begin to grasp that, compared with yours, the vast scope of our minds is confined; that the steady scale of our hearts is unsure; that the masterful skill of our hands is common.

O Spirit, like Hannah and Elkanah and Mary and Joseph, we must learn the wisdom of honoring that which lies beyond us, of keeping within our hearts that which we do not compre-

---

18 Inspired by Luke 19:41-42.

hend. Help us, as we ponder the power of your presence, the strength of your touch, and the mystery of your voice, to trust the prophets you raise up among your children and the savior you send unto your people.

*Litany*
L:   Like Hannah, the mother of Samuel, the Spirit has woven a robe for the children of God to wear:
M:   The garment is cut on the pattern of love,
W:   Which makes the two one, and unites the many.
M:   Its sleeves are made from the cloth of compassion;
W:   Its collar, from humility.
M:   Its front is fashioned from mercy and patience;
W:   Its back, from wisdom born of grief.
M:   Its sash is forgiveness, the tie that binds;
W:   Its hem is stitched with threads of kindness.
L:   Come, let us dress in the raiment of God, the saving garment, the righteous robe—
M:   Like a bridegroom decked with a garland,
W:   Like a bride adorned with jewels![19]

*Prayer for One Voice.* Great are the works of your hands, O God! They clothe you with honor and majesty, for they are faithful and just, promoting peace and sustaining iife: You make the springs to give drink to the beasts and water the trees where birds build their nests. You cause the grass to grow for pasture and sow the seed for cultivation. You fill the sea with living things and speckle the sky with eagles.

Your works cover you with a garment of light, O God, for they are righteous and good, enduring forever: You set the earth on its foundations, never to be shaken. You speak, and the mountains rise over the plain; you point, and the valleys sink to their appointed places. You order the moon to mark the seasons, and its countenance changes each passing night; you command the sun to part the days, and its face vanishes over the western horizon. You send forth your spirit, and we are created; you cry for joy, and the world is renewed.

---

19  See Isaiah 61:10.

Your works robe you in the raiment of power, O God, for they are worthy of remembrance, inspiring worship: Our praises rumble like raging waters through the mighty canyons, and soar like rushing wings toward the towering clouds, and sigh like gentle breezes through the ancient trees, and pound like galloping hooves across the windswept plains. In wisdom you have made the earth; in wisdom we shall fill the earth with rousing songs of gladness.

We will sing to you as long as we live; we will chant your praises while we have being. Like the boy Samuel, we will serve you; like the boy Jesus, we will seek you. Like both of them, we will ask the question that has been raised by your children throughout the ages, "What must we do, to be doing the works of God?" And you will answer as you have answered throughout the ages, "You shall give to others freely; you shall open wide your hands, and your hearts shall not be grudging, that I might bless you in all that you do."[20]

O one who prepared a stable for him who would have no place to lay his head, shelter us, that we might shelter others. O one who delivered him whom we would call the Great Physician, heal us, that we might heal others. O one who provided swaddling clothes for him whose robe would be gambled away, clothe us, that we might clothe others. O one who raised up teachers for him whom we would claim as our Great Teacher, guide us, that we might guide others.

Great are your works, O God, and great shall be our works if you are our Lord! Bless us, make us a faithful and just people, promoting peace and sustaining life, that the works of our hands might clothe you with honor and majesty! Make us a righteous and good people, enduring forever, that the works of our hearts might cover you with a garment of light! Make us a people worthy of remembrance, inspiring love, that the works of our spirits might robe you in the raiment of power![21]

---

20 See John 6:28; Deuteronomy 15:10-11.
21 Much imagery in this prayer has been taken from Psalm 104.

*Benediction.* As the Son of God came unto the world, let his brothers and sisters go into the world, giving thanks for life in word and deed, and growing in love for God and neighbor.

## Second Sunday After Christmas

*Lections:* Jeremiah 31:7-14; Sirach 24:1-4, 12-16 (alternate); Psalm 147:12-20; Ephesians 1:3-14; John 1:1-18

*Call to Worship*
L:  Sing aloud with gladness!
P:  Shout with great rejoicing!
L:  Proclaim the news with all your hearts,
P:  And praise the heavens with all your souls:
A:  God has saved the peoples!

*Invocation.* O Lord, like a faithful shepherd, you have gathered us from mountain and valley, from country and city, from every corner of the earth. Though we speak with different tongues and see through different eyes and cling to different beliefs, you have brought us together to understand one another.

You have made us witnesses to a nativity, with all its mystery and beauty and possibility. How could this newborn child *not* bring us together? How could he *not* turn our mourning into joy, our sorrow into gladness?

Shepherd of the world, you have, indeed, brought us into a pleasant place. Feed us in green pastures, lead us beside still waters, restore our souls![22]

*Litany*
L:  O Lord, you have freed us from hands too strong:
P:  Hands pinning us down, you have pried away;
L:  Hands pushing us apart, you have used to unite;
P:  Hands luring us toward trouble, you have pointed another way;
L:  Hands hardening into fists, you have taught to bless;
P:  Hands swinging out in rage, you have caused to clap;
L:  Hands clenching in distress, you have kneaded open;

---

22 Inspired by Psalm 23:2-3.

P:   Hands taunting in pride, you have folded in prayer;
L:   Hands hiding in pockets, you have compelled to reach out;
P:   Hands working harm, you have turned to good labor;
L:   Hands raising walls, you have made to build doors.
P:   O Lord, you have freed us from hands too strong—
L:   Some were ours; some were others'.
P:   Now *you* be the potter,
L:   And we, the clay!
P:   Make us a people of inspired works and diligent faith,
A:   With spirits made strong by your hands and hands made strong by your spirit!

*Prayer for One Voice.* O Lord, in the beginning the Word came forth from your mouth and covered the earth like a morning mist. The earth, thirsting for life, opened her lips, and as she drank, living things sprang forth—deer on the land and dolphins in the sea, birds in the sky and beasts in the field. The mist watered the whole face of the ground, until the dust no longer blew in the wind; then you formed us from the clay, and breathed into our nostrils your holy breath.[23]

This is your story, O God—the glory of your creative Word, the Living Water, the Eternal Fount. Our mouths shout your name unto the heavens; our feet dance your dance upon the earth!

O Lord, in the beginning the Word came forth from your mouth and lit up the night like the noontime sun. The earth, groping in the darkness, squinted her eyes, and as she looked, mysterious things were revealed—the beauty of her face and the bounty of her life, the brevity of eternity and the boundary of infinity. The light shone through the gloom and eclipsed every shadow, and the night waged war, but could not overcome the light.

This is your story, O God—the glory of your revealing Word, the Light of the World, the Eternal Flame. Our mouths shout your name unto the heavens; our feet dance your dance upon the earth!

O Lord, the Word was with you in the beginning of the world. And now the world has begun anew, for you have

---

23 Inspired by Genesis 2:6-7.

caused the Word to come forth again. Now the world has been reborn, for the Word has come forth from the womb of Mary. The news has wrapped the earth in an angelic hymn; it has lighted the night with a royal star.

The Word has become flesh to dwell among us, full of grace and truth. Let the Word grow, O God, and let us receive him as Living Water, that our thirst might be satisfied. Let the Word grow, and let us receive him as the Light of the World, that our hearts might be illumined. Let the Word grow, and let us receive him as the Good Shepherd, that our feet might be led where none shall stumble.

This is your story, O God—the glory of your saving Word, the Keeper of the Fold, the Eternal Friend. Our mouths shout your name unto the heavens; our feet dance your dance upon the earth!

*Benediction.* O God, let us who have been gathered together in your name not forget the pain of our separation from you and from one another. Let us remember our in-gathering, and rejoice by bringing your peace to the restless, your purpose to the aimless, and your place to the homeless.

# Season After Epiphany

(See "Celebration of Special Occasions"
for Epiphany Day.)

---

*First Sunday After Epiphany*
*Baptism of the Lord*

*Lections:* Isaiah 43:1-7; Psalm 29; Acts 8:14-17; Luke 3:15-17, 21-22

*Call to Worship*

L: God anointed Christ to console the afflicted.
P: Come, let us worship the Lord our Comforter!
L: God anointed Christ to emancipate the enslaved.
P: Come, let us worship the Lord our Liberator!
L: God anointed Christ to bind up the wounded.
P: Come, let us worship the Lord our Healer!
L: God anointed Christ to deliver the troubled.
P: Come, let us worship the Lord our Savior!

*Invocation.* O God, whose voice could dash turbulent waves against angry rocks, shoot flaming tongues across threatening skies, or blow whirling winds through helpless fields, you are the mighty Lord of heaven and earth. You are the one for whom the world waited, and you are the one for whom the world waits. Yet the sounds with which you make your presence known are rarely like the sound of rushing waters or roaring winds or raging fires. They are more like the sounds of silence—the sound of a purity so perfect, the sound of a love so selfless, the sound of a goodness so noble—sounds that move us to gasp in amazement.

Speak to us now, O Lord, in the voice with which you spoke to Jesus at his baptism. Reassure us, as you did him, that we are your beloved children, that our proclamation of the good news might be heard throughout the earth.

*Litany*

L: As Jesus asked an ancient disciple baptized in his name, so he asks us, "Do you love me?"

P: And we answer, "Lord, Lord, you know that we love you; we were baptized in your name."

L: Then Jesus says to us, "Seek the welfare of my people." And a second time he asks, "Do you love me?"

P: Then again we answer, "Lord, Lord, you know that we love you; we were baptized in your name."

L: Then Jesus says to us, "Minister to the needs of my people." And still a third time he asks, "Do you love me?"

P: Once again we answer, "Lord, Lord, you know that we love you; we were baptized in your name."

L: And Jesus says to us, "Then serve my people. Not all who say, 'Lord, Lord,' shall enter the kingdom of heaven, but only they who do the will of God."

*Prayer for One Voice.* Almighty and eternal God, Lord of Christ, we bow before you in honor of him who for our sake became one of us that we might become one with you. Before his coming, O God, we most often listened for your voice in the startling sounds of nature in upheaval—the crack of lightning, the blast of thunder, the roar of the tornado, the explosion of the volcano, the whip of the hurricane.

But now, thanks to him, we have no excuse for being surprised when your voice comes to us in hushed tones—claiming us as your children, directing us to your task, humbling us in our strength, and consoling us in our weakness. Thanks to him, we have no excuse for ignoring your affirmation of us at our baptism, or for reducing the meaning of baptism to the words of a prescribed ritual. Let us not forget, O Lord, that our public acknowledgment of kinship with you must ever be matched by the private; that the outward sign must ever be matched by the inward change it signifies; that the holy sacrament must ever be matched by holy living.

We know, O Lord, that you do not address us as your beloved children lightly or unadvisedly. You did not greet Jesus as your child because others pinned on him the lofty title of Messiah, but because he embraced the lowly task of your servant. And you will not so greet us until we claim his mission as enthusiastically as we claim his name, until the decision to take the name of Jesus with us is joined by the determination to take the love of Jesus with us. For the sake of your people and ours, and for the sake of your joy and ours, we ask, O Lord, for the courage to honor faithfully the Christ whose name we so often take in vain.

When we survey the world around us, we behold a sea of faces troubled by a world in fateful transition, faces anxious for some assurance that there is meaning in the struggle. Grant us the grace, O God, so to proclaim your message of meaning that the troubled world will be comforted, the anxious consoled. Let us proclaim your message not by echoing a heavenly voice but by performing earthly deeds; not by gazing at openings in the sky but by seizing opportunities on the ground; not simply by calling for reliance on the Holy Spirit but by acting in reliance on the Holy Spirit; not simply by inviting divine intervention but by implementing human intention.

As we have been baptized in the name of Jesus Christ, baptize us now, O Lord, in the *cause* of Jesus Christ, until his mission becomes our mission and we perform it in his spirit.

*Benediction.* Go now in the assurance that the spirit with which God anointed Christ is the spirit with which God anoints us; that the mission to which God called Christ is the mission to which God calls us; that the power with which God strengthened Christ is the power with which God strengthens us; and that the love with which God transformed the world through Christ can be ours and the world's for the sharing.

## Second Sunday After Epiphany

*Lections*: Isaiah 62:1-5; Psalm 36:5-10; I Corinthians 12:1-11; John 2:1-11

### Call to Worship

L: Are you troubled by the fickleness of human love?
P: Come and worship the Lord, whose love is faithful.
L: Are you troubled by the harshness of human judgments?
P: Come and worship the Lord, whose judgments are healing.

L: Are you troubled by the pride of human righteousness?
P: Come, let us worship the Lord, whose righteousness is pure.
A: Let us praise the Lord our God, whose love can make us faithful, whose judgments can make us whole, and whose righteousness can make us pure.

*Invocation.* O Christ, our Lord and Savior, from whose waters the faint can drink and never thirst again; beneath whose wings the homeless can take refuge and never fear again; on whose abundance the hungry can feed and never want again, we turn to you now, because there is no other to whom we can turn. We have tried other fountains, only to thirst again; other havens, only to fear again; and other homes, only to want again. And so, chastened by the betrayal of our false messiahs, we return to you, O Christ, in confidence and hope.

*Litany*

L: O God, whose spirit blesses us with many and various gifts,
P: Help us to stress not the diversity of our gifts but the unity of their source.
L: If we have more or greater gifts than others,
P: Let us not boast, for all our gifts are given by you for the good of all.
L: If our neighbors have more or greater gifts than we,
P: Let us not grumble, for all their gifts are given by you for the good of all.
L: If we have tasks too big for our gifts,
P: Let us not be quick to spurn the help of others.
L: If our neighbors have gifts that are too small for their tasks,
P: Let us not be slow to offer our help to others.
L: As Christ employed his gifts to manifest your spirit,
A: Help us to employ our gifts to manifest the spirit of Christ.

*Prayer for One Voice.* O Lord, Vindicator of the abused, Redeemer of the oppressed, Refuge of the exiled, and Fortress of the besieged, we call you by all these names because we have experienced you in all these ways. When we were abused, you vindicated us; when we were oppressed, you redeemed us; when we were exiled, you sheltered us; and when we were besieged, you strengthened us. So we address you now, O God, as in times past our ancestors addressed you.

Your detractors would have us believe that we give you more credit than you are due. Determined to topple you from the throne of life, they call the roll of human beings who have justified us, set us free, made us safe, and kept us strong. Too captivated by human achievement to consider its source, they do not see you, unless you blind them with the rays of the noonday sun; they do not hear you, unless you deafen them with the roar of a waterfall; they do not feel you, unless you sweep them aside with the winds of a blizzard. But we know better, Lord: We do not look for you only in the sights that dazzle; we do not listen for you only in the sounds that deafen; we do not feel you only in the forces that overwhelm. We remember in whose image we are created, and we believe the presence that cannot be seen; we listen to the voice that cannot be heard; we grasp the hand that cannot be touched. We thank you, dear Lord, for delivering us from the skepticism that denies you because it cannot prove you, and from the dogmatism that affirms you because it *can* prove you.

When we consider the gifts with which you blessed the world though Jesus—concern for the weak and afflicted, compassion for the sick and imprisoned, love for the lowly and despised—we are amazed by how many of them are within our reach. You have made us but a little lower than yourself; you have set eternity within the heart of each of us and made the incarnation of your spirit a possibility for all of us. Yet your clear light, the light that shone so brilliantly yet so modestly in Jesus, condemns us even as it instructs us. Unlike Jesus, we seek not so much to serve as to impress our neighbors. As much as we might like to help others discover their gifts, we prefer to win praise by displaying our own. So the gifts that were meant to tie us together work to tear us apart, and our unity in diversity becomes bitterness in division.

O God, we turn to you in confession and supplication. Before you and our neighbors, we acknowledge our abuse of your gifts. Forgive us for exercising them without respect for your purpose in bestowing them. Help us to recognize that you call us to use our gifts—not that others might conceal theirs, but that others might reveal theirs; not that the abilities of some might be applauded, but that the abilities of all might be appreciated; not that the worth of individuals might be downgraded, but that the welfare of the community might be upgraded.

Dear Lord, we are especially mindful of those in the human community whose struggle for existence is so dominated by concern for clothing and shelter and bread that it has yet to become a struggle for meaning. Let us never forget that they are no less your children than we and that, just as you have blessed us with diverse gifts, so you have blessed them. So we pray that you will enable us to help them discover their gifts, that they might use them in your spirit for the common good.

*Benediction.* O God, as you are called a new name because of the life of Jesus Christ, we are called Christians because of our membership in Christ's church. Grant that, even as his words and deeds have brought glory to your name, our words and deeds shall bring glory to his name.

## Third Sunday After Epiphany

*Lections*: Nehemiah 8:1-3, 5-6, 8-10; Psalm 19; I Corinthians 12:12-31*a*; Luke 4:14-21

*Call to Worship*

L:  Come, let us worship the Lord,
P:  Whose law revives the soul.
L:  Come, let us worship the Lord,
P:  Whose testimony instructs the mind.
L:  Come, let us worship the Lord,
P:  Whose precepts gladden the heart.
L:  Come, let us worship the Lord,
A:  And the Lord our God shall bless us!

*Invocation.* O God, we come together to explore the meaning of our membership in the body of Christ. As we examine ourselves, keep ever before us the example of him whom you appointed the head of the body. So guide our reflection on the life of Jesus that we might find your purpose for ours.

*Litany*

L:  O God, when you delivered us from Egyptian bondage, Moses called us together at Sinai,

P:  And there he proclaimed your mighty deeds and set before us your solemn demands.

L:  Then the two became one: The Lord, the God of Israel; and Israel, the people of the Lord.

P:  And then, even though we wandered in the wilderness, we did not wander as sheep without a shepherd.

A:  The Lord was our shepherd!

L:  O God, when you delivered us from Babylonian bondage, Ezra called us together in Jerusalem,

P:  And there he proclaimed your mighty deeds and set before us your solemn demands.

L:  Then the two became one: The Lord, the God of the Jews; and the Jews, the people of God.

P:  And then, even though we were scattered throughout the earth, we did not wander as sheep without a shepherd.

A:  The Lord was our shepherd!

L:  O God, when you redeemed us from the bondage of sin, Jesus called us together on the Mount,

P:  And there he proclaimed your mighty deeds and set before us your solemn demands.

L:  And then the two became one: Christ, the head of the church; and the church, the body of Christ.

P:  And now, even when we are forced to wander in strange lands, we do not wander as sheep without a shepherd.

A:  The Lord is our shepherd!

*Prayer for One Voice.* O God, whose majesty fills the heavens with glory and whose love floods the earth with meaning, we approach you in awe and gratitude, giving thanks that we are made in your image, called according to your purpose, and commissioned to do your will.

At times, we are overwhelmed by the difficulty of this commission. The distance between you and us is so great! But you never leave us without help. You bless us with guides and with guidance, sending into our midst lawgivers, prophets, priests, psalmists, sages, apostles, and missionaries. And you make *us* your witnesses, that we might revive the soul of the church, even as your law once revived the soul of Israel. We pray that, just as your guidance enabled Israel to fulfill her commission, it might now enable us to fulfill ours.

Forgive us, O Lord, for the selfish way we often accept your help. We are quick to claim your healing for our broken hearts, but slow to extend it to others; we are impatient to demand your release from whatever holds us captive, but reluctant to proclaim release for our neighbors; we are bold to assert our right to the satisfaction of our material needs, but content to spiritualize the needs of others. We dismiss the critics who equate the church with the noise of our solemn assemblies, but we do not provide them with much evidence to the contrary. We do not hesitate to call ourselves the body of Christ, but we do hesitate to embrace Christ's mission. For this, O God, we acknowledge our sin against you, against our neighbors, and against ourselves. And we pray that, just as you come to us at our point of need, you will send us to others at their point of need.

Set us on a course that will lead us to discover gifts we never knew we had and to use them in behalf of people we never knew were there: the poor, the bound, the afflicted, the oppressed, the homeless, the helpless, and the hopeless—the very people in whose service Jesus found the key to his mission and ours. Deliver us from the paternalism that permits us to think less highly of them than we ought. And save us from the individualism that allows us never to think of them at all. As your spirit indwelled the body of the man from Nazareth, let it now indwell your body of believers, so that, when one member rejoices, all will rejoice; when one member suffers, all will suffer; and when one member slips, all will jump to the rescue.

O God, who sent Christ to be the light of the world and the light for the world, shine within us, upon us, around us. When we ignore the people Christ came to serve, illumine our hearts, lest we mistake our selfishness for your indifference. When we ignore the prophets you send to speak, illumine our minds, lest we apply yesterday's solutions to today's problems. When we ignore the commandments you deliver to inspire, illumine our wills, lest we substitute correct ideas for constructive action.

41

Let all who walk in darkness behold in Christ's body of believers the same light that others who walked in darkness beheld in Jesus.

*Benediction*

L: O Christ, you have blessed the members of your body with many and diverse gifts.

P: Now send us forth to bear witness to the oneness of our God and the unity of your church.

L: You have given none of us all the gifts for bringing your kingdom to earth.

P: But you *have* given each of us some gift for bringing your kingdom to earth.

L: Therefore let us not hold back, lamenting the gifts we do not have;

A: But let us press ahead, employing the gifts we do have.

## Fourth Sunday After Epiphany

*Lections*: Jeremiah 1:4-10; Psalm 71:1-6; I Corinthians 13:1-13; Luke 4:21-30

*Call to Worship*

L: From a world in which injustice sits upon the throne,

P: We turn to you, O Lord, our refuge from workers of woe.

L: With hearts from which courage has taken leave,

P: We turn to you, O Lord, our refuge from dealers in fear.

L: We have hewn out for ourselves broken cisterns that can hold no water.[24]

P: Now we turn to you, O Lord, the fountain of living water,

A: That courage might rule our hearts and justice cover the earth.

*Invocation*. Gracious God, in Jesus Christ you introduced yourself as the help of the hopeless and the hope of the helpless, and you called us to proclaim your name and portray your character. With gladness we heeded your summons. But our enthusiasm has waned, and your mission has suffered. So we pray, O Lord, for the renewal of our vision of Jesus Christ, that our enthusiasm

---

24 See Jeremiah 2:13.

for his mission might be rekindled and that, once again, the helpless might find hope and the hopeless might find help.

*Litany*

L: O God, when the world grows weary of our righteous confessions and rigid creeds,

P: Help us to remember that Jesus did not go about talking big but doing good.

L: When the world grows weary of our date-setting speculations and doomsday prophecies,

P: Help us to remember that Jesus did not go about chasing mysteries but confronting realities.

L: When the world grows weary of our sterile knowledge and our strident doctrines,

P: Help us to remember that Jesus did not go about defending propositions but speaking parables.

L: When the world grows weary of our clannish nationalism and religious parochialism,

P: Help us to remember that Jesus did not go about coddling bigotry but demanding charity.

L: When the world grows weary of our childish beliefs and otherworldly concerns,

P: Help us to remember that Jesus did not go about pondering eternity but practicing love.

A: So faith, hope, and love abide; but the greatest of these is love.[25]

*Prayer for One Voice.* Gracious God, our Lord and Savior, we turn to you in grateful confidence, for you are no stranger to us. Were it not for you, you *could* be a stranger. We do our best to put distance between you and ourselves, but you are better at bringing us together than we are at keeping us apart. You confront us with a power we cannot manipulate, a goodness we cannot match, a love we cannot deny; for this, dear Lord, we bless you and pray for your blessing upon us. Let your power become to us not merely an object of awe but a source of renewal; let your goodness become to us not merely a thing of envy but a model for life; let your love become to us not merely

---

25 See I Corinthians 13:13.

an inescapable force but a contagious presence, that we might remember not only to whom we should give thanks, but why.

We voice this plea, O Lord, with hesitation. Not that we doubt your intentions or your ability to accomplish them. We know that before we move in love toward you, you have already moved in love toward us; before we seek you, you have already sought us. Nevertheless, we do hesitate, for we are saddled with memories—vivid memories, bitter memories—of the times we failed to conform our action to your intention: when those in life's quicksand might have been rescued, but we did not extend a helping hand; when the cause of justice might have been advanced, but we did not plead its case; when the obstacles to a healthy environment might have been re-moved, but we did not lend our strength. We would like to forget: the times you said to pluck up, and we continued to plant; the times you said to go here, and we went there; the times you said to do this, and we did that; the times you said to speak boldly, and we spoke timidly, if at all.

When we review these times, we are astounded, O Lord, that you remain near to hear us and to receive us and to forgive us; that you stand ready, even though we repeatedly make you our second choice, to offer us a second chance. So we approach you in repentance and hope, chastened by your ability to remember, yet encouraged by your readiness to forget.

O God, turn our eyes from our unalterable past to our open future: from the hateful words we have spoken to the healing words we yet can speak; from the thoughtless deeds we have done to the thoughtful deeds we yet can do; from the worthless causes we have supported to the worthwhile causes we yet can support; from the uncaring society we have shaped to the caring society we yet can shape.

O Lord, the world is full of people we yet can help. Open our eyes, that we might see them; our hearts, that we might love them; our mouths, that we might defend them; and our hands, that we might assist them, as together we seek to discern and do your will, through Jesus Christ our Lord.

*Benediction.* O Lord, as you have become our refuge from the world's injustice, send us into the world to become a refuge for its victims. Let your light so illumine us that they not only might discover the path to peace with justice, but find the courage to make it a highway.

## Fifth Sunday After Epiphany

*Lections*: Isaiah 6:1-8 (9-13); Psalm 138; I Corinthians 15:1-11; Luke 5:1-11

### Call to Worship
L: At a time when rulers are shouting threats, a mighty chorus ever swelling,
P: Holy, holy is the Lord, their idle boasts dispelling!
L: So we come together in Christ's name, the spirit with us dwelling,
A: And join the choirs of heaven and earth, our humble praises telling!

*Invocation.* O God, whose majesty rules the heavens above and whose glory fills the earth below, whose goodness no saint can approach and whose grace no sinner can defeat, we come together to acknowledge your majesty and rejoice in your glory, to affirm your goodness and claim your grace. Deliver us, dear Lord, as we bow before you in prayer, from pride in our achievements and from guilt over our transgressions, so that, in humble faith and with pure hearts, we might worship you in truth and serve you in love.

### Litany
L: O Lord, when our leaders make decisions that move our hearts to doubt,
P: We turn to you, the ruler of heaven, in whom we can surely trust.
L: We behold in you the power that causes the weak to be strengthened;
P: We behold in you the grace that causes the proud to be humbled.
L: Remove the sin that festers around us and within us;
P: We look to you, O ruler of heaven, for forgiveness and acceptance.

45

L: Place your merciful touch on our lips, and let your summons fall upon our ears;

P: We look to you, O ruler of heaven, for inspiration and guidance.

L: If you must, offend our hearing and confuse our understanding;

P: We look to you, O ruler of heaven, for revelation and commission.

L: Stand with us, O God, in our hour of trial, as you stood with Jesus in his;

P: We turn to you, O ruler of heaven, in whom we can surely trust.

*Prayer for One Voice.* Almighty and gracious God, who towers over us with such majesty that we cannot but acknowledge our insignificance, and yet who draws close to us with such mercy that we cannot *deny* our *significance,* we adore you. We adore you for who and what you are. And we thank you for who and what *we* are—and for who and what we can become.

We are grateful, O Lord, for your self-disclosure in Jesus of Nazareth—not because he was so unlike us, but because he was so like you: so like you that we could look at him and see you, we could listen to him and hear you; so like you that we could read his mind and know yours, we could learn his will and obey yours. Yes, Lord, we thank you for Jesus Christ, the revealer of you to us and of us to you.

We also thank you for all those who keep the vision of him vivid and the spirit of him vital: those who, launching their search for you, study his journey with you; those who, seeking your will for them, ponder your guidance of him; those who, confronting the snares of temptation, examine his rebuke of the Tempter; those who, living in the shadow of suffering, remember his victory over Calvary. We owe such a great debt to these people that we can never repay it. Yet we can live and labor, as did they, to reclaim the vision and revive the spirit of Jesus Christ.

For this to happen, O God, the story of our lives must take a new direction. Our story has been of peaks and valleys, with too many valleys and too few peaks. Again and again you have called us to take the high ground, but found us content to settle for the low ground: more anxious to keep the friendship of the privileged than to secure the rights of the disadvantaged; more ready to appease the mighty than to applaud the merciful; more willing, in the struggle for justice, to sit on the sidelines than to stand in the frontlines; more concerned to guarantee the fortunes of our people than to enrich the future of your people; more disposed to claim your support of our causes than to risk our support of your cause.

As we review this story, we bow in shame and in hope—in shame, knowing that we could have written a different story; yet in hope, knowing that, as we write its new chapters, we can count on your help. We pray, dear Lord, that you will make the story of our lives not only different but better—a story of which neither you nor we need be ashamed.

Like Paul, we are among the untimely born. Nevertheless, we pray that you will enable us, like him, to perceive and to mediate the presence of Christ. Deliver us from all the habits of mind and heart and conduct that might hide Christ from our neighbors. Grant us the grace so to represent Christ that his appearances will continue without end.

*Benediction*

L:  We were glad, O Christ, when you called us together for worship in your house.

P:  Now make us glad as we go apart for service in your world.

A:  As you brought us together to praise your name, send us forth to manifest your spirit.

## Sixth Sunday After Epiphany
*(If this is Last Sunday After Epiphany, see p. 54.)*

*Lections*: Jeremiah 17:5-10; Psalm 1; I Corinthians 15:12-20; Luke 6:17-26

*Call to Worship*

L:  Rejoice, for the power of God has come—

P:  The same transforming power encountered in the risen Christ:

L:  Promising to the poor the realm of heaven;

P:  Promising to the hungry a time of satisfaction;

L:  Promising to the weeping a life of happiness;

P:  Promising to the reviled the gift of acceptance.
A:  Rejoice, O people of God, the transforming power of
    Christ is here!

*Invocation.* O Christ, whom even crucifixion could not separate
from either the love or the power of God, bless us, the members
of your body, with the guidance of your spirit, that we might seek
God with your singleness of mind, see God with your clarity of
understanding, and worship God with your purity of heart.

*Litany*
L:  O Christ, compel us to reexamine the standards by which
    we judge—
P:  The values we condone, the values by which we condemn.
L:  You pronounce blessings upon the poor and the hungry;
P:  If you be for them, shall we dare be against them?
L:  You pronounce blessings upon the weeping and the forsaken;
P:  If you be for them, shall we dare be against them?
L:  You pronounce woes upon the greedy and the pretentious;
P:  If you be against them, shall we dare be for them?
L:  You pronounce woes upon the proud and the deceitful;
P:  If you be against them, shall we dare be for them?
L:  O Christ, inspire us to embrace the standards by which
    *you* judge—
P:  The values by which you favor, the values by which you forgive!

*Prayer for One Voice.* Gracious Lord and Savior, whose spirit
guided Jesus in life and glorified him in death, we adore you
for coming to us in him and for leading us to you through him.

As the time between his life and ours grows longer, we are
forced to turn to others for our knowledge of him: to the
shapers of the traditions about him; the collectors of the stories
about his life and teaching; and the commentators who,
through the centuries, have related the Lord of the ages to the
needs of the age. Often these guardians of the faith have kept
it alive and relevant at great personal sacrifice and risk. To
them we owe a debt of endless appreciation and gratitude.

And not only to them do we owe this debt, but also to those
in whose lives we have beheld the likeness of Jesus. Their
names may not be found on the covers of books or even on the

pages between. Yet they are the people who come to mind when we ask what Jesus would do in our situation; what you would have us do at a given moment; whether we should take this side or that; how we can most usefully invest our energies and abilities. All of us have known them, and just now, O God, we pay tribute to the beauty of their lives and the influence of their lives on ours. By their example, they have taught us afresh what it means for the Word to become flesh.

Yet our appreciation of them is blunted by the painful awareness of how often we ignore their wise counsel; how rarely we follow their good example; how little we treasure their low regard for things; how casually we dismiss their genuine respect for persons; how lightly we take their unswerving commitment to personal integrity; how easily we betray their passion for social justice.

We cannot undo the mistakes of the past, O God, but you can spare us their repetition. Make clear to us when we are putting our trust in persons who do not put their trust in you. Try our hearts, lest we substitute loyalty to human beings for loyalty to you. As we look to Jesus, through whom you made yourself real to those who made Jesus real for us, grant us the grace to follow in their footsteps. Help us to become to others what they have become to us: prophets of peace and apostles of justice.

*Benediction.* In this place of worship, we have proclaimed the presence and power of the risen Christ with the words of our mouths and the meditations of our hearts. Now, as we go forth to our places of work, let us demonstrate the presence and power of the risen Christ with the deeds of our hands and the labors of our lives.

### *Seventh Sunday After Epiphany*
*(If this is Last Sunday After Epiphany, see p. 54.)*

*Lections*: Genesis 45:3-11, 15; Psalm 37:1-11, 39-40; I Corinthians 15:35-38, 42-50; Luke 6:27-38

# LITANIES AND OTHER PRAYERS

*Call to Worship*

L: As the sons of Jacob and Rachel betrayed their brother Joseph,

P: We, your daughters and sons, have betrayed you, O Lord.

L: And, as they were welcomed and forgiven by Joseph,

P: We are forgiven and welcomed by you.

L: So now we come into your presence, O Lord—

A: To accept your pardon and receive your mercy.

*Invocation.* O God, who turned the abused into the Savior of the abusers and the crucified into the Redeemer of the crucifiers, we thank you for the miracle of your transforming presence in Jesus Christ. Grant us the grace so to contemplate that miracle that it might be repeated in us. And deliver us from the temptation either to diminish the power of your manifestation in him or to dismiss the possibility of your manifestation in us.

*Litany*

L: Blessed are we not when we do unto others as they would do unto us,

P: But when we do unto others as the Lord would do unto us:

L: Not when we look around at the example of our neighbors,

P: But when we look back to the life of the Nazarene—

L: Who warns us against helping only those who can give us something in return,

P: And bids us help those who can give us nothing in return;

L: Who counsels us against trimming gifts to the demands of those who ask,

P: And challenges us to give, instead, according to their needs;

L: Who denies us special credit for loving those who love us,

P: And commends us for loving those who make it hard to love;

L: Who cautions us against wreaking vengeance upon our enemies,

P: And summons us to be merciful to the pitiless and the proud.

L: O Christ, you have shown us the way to love God and serve our neighbors;

P: Let your life be a light unto our feet and a beacon unto our hearts.

*Prayer for One Voice.* Gracious God, who endows earthly inhabitants with heavenly dreams and tests mortal limits with immortal longings, you never cease to amaze and confound us. You make life possible, but you also make life unpredictable. For while you create us in your image, filling us with aspirations that only you can satisfy, you grant us our freedom, confronting us with choices that only we can make. You make us creatures of dignity, and you treat us accordingly. You initiate a covenant with us, but you leave it unsealed until we accept it in faith. You could win our acceptance by coercion, but you seek it by choice. You do not rely on the manipulation of your awesome might but on the manifestation of your suffering love; not on superior strength but on amazing grace; not on the power to inflict pain upon us but on the power to endure pain for us. So we thank you, dear Lord, not only for being the God whose image we behold in Jesus, but for being the God who, in Jesus, beholds our image.

O God, who in Christ calls us to conform our lives to your will, we acknowledge our failure to heed this summons. Time and again, even though mindful of his ways, we have not walked in Christ's steps. We knew of his readiness to help those who could not help him, yet we have restricted our help to those who can help us. We knew of his willingness to give to those who could not give to him, yet we have given only to those who can give to us. We knew of his quickness to forgive his enemies, yet we have been slow to forgive even our friends. Forgive us, dear Lord, for our betrayal of your summons. Draw us nearer to yourself, that we might find the desire to discern your will and the strength to do it.

O Lord, as we behold spirited multitudes emerging from long years of bleak oppression, help us to surround them with your spirit; to reassure them of your love and of our readiness, as your agents, to assist them in their struggle for freedom with dignity, order with justice, and peace with honor.

A tumult of voices is calling us, Lord, but only yours is calling us to give hope to the hopeless, help to the helpless, comfort to the friendless, and meaning to the aimless. Help us, amidst all these voices, not only to distinguish yours from all others, but to heed yours above all others.

*Benediction.* O Christ, help us to be your disciples in deed and in truth. Grant us the grace to bless those who curse us, to forgive those who condemn us, to receive those who judge us, and to love those who hate us. Thus do we pray, that all your people might be one in the spirit as in the flesh.

## Eighth Sunday After Epiphany
### (If this is Last Sunday After Epiphany, see p. 54.)

*Lections*: Sirach 27:4-7; Isaiah 55:10-13 (alternate); Psalm 92:1-4, 12-15; I Corinthians 15:51-58; Luke 6:39-49

### Call to Worship
L:  Come unto me, says the Lord, that I may be your God and you may be my people:
P:  Though our minds be clouded with thoughts of self, they shall find room for thoughts of others;
L:  Though our souls be set on private gain, they shall find release for the public good;
P:  Though our hearts be burdened with feelings of guilt, they shall find joy in the gift of forgiveness.
A:  Come unto us, O Lord, that you might be our God and we might be your people.[26]

*Invocation.* O Christ, as in your presence we have gathered to seek your direction, prepare us to receive your guidance. Unstop our ears, that we might distinguish the sound of your voice. Open our eyes, that we might read the signal of your hand. Loosen our tongues, that we might proclaim the beauty of your holiness. And quicken our hearts, that we might repeat the glory of your obedience.

### Litany
L:  O let us arise to give thanks to the Lord,
P:  Who promises to join us when we gather in Christ's name.
L:  Let not our words of praise be so many idle words,
P:  Crying, "Lord, Lord," to the heavens, but refusing to do God's will.

---

26  Inspired by Isaiah 1:18.

L: Let us be doers and not just hearers of the word,

P: Doing unto others as we would have them do unto us.

L: Let us be known by our deeds, as trees are known by their fruits,

P: For noble deeds come from noble hearts, as good fruit from good trees.

L: Let us ask the Lord to create within us a clean and upright heart—[27]

P: Then we shall offer thanks and praise, and the Lord will hear our prayer!

*Prayer for One Voice.* O God, who has made us in your image, so that we cannot know the life you intend for us until you live in us and we in you, we thank you for the gift of life. We thank you for our life as human beings, the life that sets us apart from all the rest of your creation. We thank you for our life as people of the covenant, the life that sets us apart as your agents for the restoration of all creation. We thank you for our life as members of the body of Christ, the life that sets us apart for the sharing of life as you mean it to be.

Thanks to Jesus Christ, we seek you with knowledge of who you are. Not only has he taught us that we must think your thoughts; he has thought your thoughts. Not only has he taught us that we must feel your feelings; he has felt your feelings. Not only has he taught us that we must do your deeds; he has done your deeds. We do not know you as you know us, but thanks be to Jesus Christ, we know you too well to excuse ourselves for not being more like you.

And we know you too well to think that you do not know us for who we are: persons who long to reap the harvest of love but sow the seeds of hate; who aspire to build bridges to peace but beat the paths of discord; who intend to fill the stomachs of the needy but line the pockets of the greedy; who claim to stand for the cause of justice but bow before the wave of injustice. O Lord, we confess before you and before the world that we are not the people we would like to be, nor the people you would have us be. But where there is life, there is hope,

---

27 See Matthew 18:20; Psalm 51:9.

and we are yet alive. And where there is Christ, there is redemption, and Christ is forever among us.

We pray, O God, that, as you have given Christ a glorious body, immortal and imperishable, you will confirm our membership in that body. As he thought your thoughts until he could feel your feelings and do your deeds, enable us to think his thoughts until *we* can feel *his* feelings and do *his* deeds. Deliver us from the self-defeating notion that you cannot work the same works, and even greater works, through his body of believers that you wrought through his body of flesh and blood. Let us not forget that the same spirit that animated his earthly body is alive and at work in his new body, seeking to emancipate us from our past and stamp your claim on our future.

We think now of all those who turn to us in search of you. As the moisture of the heavens nourishes the plants of the earth, let your word bring to glorious harvest the seeds of truth and righteousness in our lives. Help us to confront our neighbors with a harmony between word and deed that inspires confidence. If we impress them, let it be not with the words of our lips but with the works of our lives; not with our holy rhetoric but with our humble resolve; not with our splendid acts of worship but with our gentle acts of mercy. O Lord, let them remember, and let us not forget, that it is for their sake, not our own, that we are sanctified.

*Benediction.* O Lord, as with joy we have gathered to sing your praise, let us now scatter to do your will. You have been quick to minister to our needs; make us quick to minister to the needs of others, that our lives might bear fruit for you in the church and in the world.

## Last Sunday After Epiphany
### Transfiguration Sunday

*Lections*: Exodus 34:29-35; Psalm 99; II Corinthians 3:12-13 (14-15), 3:16–4:2; Luke 9:28-36 (37-43)

*Call to Worship*
L:    The Lord our God is a holy God.

P: Let us be holy, for the Lord our God is holy.
L: The Lord our God is a just God.
P: Let us be just, for the Lord our God is just.
L: The Lord our God is a righteous God.
P: Let us be righteous, for the Lord our God is righteous.
L: The Lord our God is a jealous God.
P: Let us worship the Lord our God, for there is no God but the Lord!

*Invocation.* O God, you reveal yourself and declare your will to people in every age. We come unto you now as have our forebears, seeking the gift of your countenance and the guidance of your spirit. But we do not come alone. We bring with us the likenesses of all the false gods to whom we have bowed our knee, of all the false prophets to whom we have inclined our ear.

O Lord, break down the temples of all these alien deities, and deliver us from all their agents. And let us hear again the voice that said of Jesus, "This is my Chosen; to this one you shall listen!"

*Litany*
L: The Lord reigns; let the earth rejoice and be glad!
P: Go, tell everybody everywhere that Jesus Christ is Lord!
L: Go, tell the haughty that they shall be brought low,
P: And the lowly that they shall be lifted up.
L: Go, tell the well that they shall become ill,
P: And the ill that they shall be made well.
L: Go, tell the rich that they shall become poor,
P: And the poor that they shall become rich.
L: Go, tell the oppressors that they shall be enslaved,
P: And the oppressed that they shall be set free.
L: Go, tell the strong that they shall become weak,
P: And the weak that they shall become strong.
L: Go, tell the first that they shall be last,
P: And the last that they shall be first.
L: Go, tell everybody everywhere that Jesus Christ is Lord—
P: That he has turned the world upside down,

A:  And the kingdoms of this world shall become the kingdom of God.[28]

*Prayer for One Voice.* Gracious God, who knows our weaknesses
before we indulge them and meets our needs before we voice
them, you are a great and mighty God, Ruler of rulers and Lord
of lords. When we consider the distance between us—between
you, the only truly Holy One, and ourselves, the very truly
human ones—we should be traumatized by fear and reduced
to silence. Yet we are not consumed by fear, and we dare to
open our mouths as well as our hearts. We enter your presence
with joy and thanksgiving, and we speak our minds with
confidence and boldness. We approach you not because of who
we are, but because of who you are; not because of what we do
for you, but because of what you do for us; not because of the
obedience with which we serve you, but because of the love
with which you seek us.

So we come before you, O Lord, secure in the faith that, even
though we deserve abandonment, you will never abandon us;
that even though we can never merit your love, you will always
love us. You will never stop trying to make us worthy of your
adoration, to incline our hearts to your will, to set our feet on
the path to peace and justice. For this love—a love that demands obedience, yet woos the disobedient—we are grateful,
and by this love we are humbled.

Indeed, when we consider its cost, we are humiliated. We
see your love walking the shores of Galilee, speaking comforting words to the lowly, only to be met by indignant cries from
the mighty. We see your love moving into a ditch beside the
Jericho Road, rescuing the victim of highway robbery, only to
be chastised for risking travel in a dangerous land. We see your
love chatting with a Samaritan woman, aware of her transgressions yet not condemning her, only to be censored by the pious
for moral indifference.

Yes, Lord, we are humiliated by your love, for we help to
drive up its cost. When the lowly are comforted, we are as apt
to speak words of indignation as of approval; when the victims

---

28  Inspired by Acts 17:6; Revelation 11:15.

of crime are aided, we are as apt to defend the cautious as to applaud the compassionate; and when sinners are transformed by the love of their neighbors, we are as apt to condemn the neighbors for the company they kept as to commend the sinners for the change they made. Forgive us, O God, for claiming for ourselves a grace that we deny to others. Deliver us from the hypocrisy of our ways, that they who look to us for compassion shall no longer turn from us in frustration.

Gracious God, who in Jesus Christ has commended yourself to us, enable us so to walk among our neighbors that we shall commend Jesus Christ to them. Let us remember, when they turn to us, to direct them to your Chosen, the one of whom you say, "This is my Son; listen to him!"

*Benediction.* O Lord, whose passion for justice is offended by injustice, whose love for right is offended by wrong, and whose concern for equity is offended by inequity, send us forth so committed to you that your will and our will shall become one. Help us so to live that we no longer offend your concern for equity, your love for right, or your passion for justice.

# Lenten Season

---

### Ash Wednesday

*Lections:* Joel 2:1-2, 12-17*a*; Psalm 51:1-17; II Corinthians 5:20*b*–6:10; Matthew 6:1-6, 16-21

*Call to Worship*
L:   The day of the Lord is coming! The day of the Lord is near!
P:   The time is fulfilled! The reign of God is at hand![29]
L:   O people, repent! Believe in the gospel!
P:   Come, let us turn and follow the Lord!

*Invocation.* Where *are* you, O God? We are lost in the night; have you cast us from your presence? Temptations surround us; their masks grin through the darkness. We run from them, but which way should we go? Where can we hide when all lies in shadow?

Have mercy on us, O God. Our eyes are swollen from tears; our bones are cold with fear; our souls have been broken—do you not *hear*, Lord?[30]

Save us! According to your steadfast love, answer us![31] Do not hide your face, but draw near, and redeem us!

*Litany*
L:   O Lord, you desire truth in our inward being;
P:   Teach us wisdom in our secret heart.
L:   Send out your light, send out your truth,
P:   And let them lead us to our home.[32]
L:   Take from us the weight of our sin,
P:   That room might be made for the spirit of truth.
L:   Hearts laden with guilt cannot receive her;
P:   They neither see nor know the glory of her grace.[33]
L:   But if we prepare a dwelling place, she will abide within us,

---

29  See Mark 1:15.
30  Inspired by Psalm 31:9-10.
31  See Psalm 69:13-14.
32  See Psalm 43:3*a*.
33  Inspired by John 1:14.

L: But if we prepare a dwelling place, she will abide within us,
P: And the truth will set our spirits free.
L: Then shall we love not only in word or in speech; then shall we love in deed and in truth,
P: And by this know that our service is faithful.[34]
L: O Lord, you desire truth in our inward being;
P: Teach us wisdom in our secret heart.

*Prayer for One Voice.* O Lord, you have appeared among us, but we have not seen you. You have walked among us, but we have not followed you. You have spoken among us, but we have not understood you. You have rejoiced among us, but we have not embraced you.[35] You have suffered among us, but we have not saved you.

We looked for your coming for so long, O Lord! But, with our eyes fastened on the horizon, we missed your approach—until now. Now we see that your day is near, near and hastening fast: a day of distress and anguish, a day of ruin and devastation, a day of clouds and gloom; a day when we shall grope in the blindness of our sin, and our silver and gold shall fail us.[36]

Now, O Lord, we see that your day is near! The earth mourns and withers, and the heavens languish with her. The earth lies polluted beneath us, a curse devours her; she is utterly broken, rent asunder. Staggering under her burdens like a drunkard, she collapses and will not rise again.[37]

Now, O Lord, we see that your day is near! And how we tremble in repentance, we who have violated heaven and earth, who suffer for their pain! How we long for your abundant mercy! Appear again among us, and this time we will see. Walk again among us, and this time we will follow. Speak again among us, and this time we will understand. Rejoice again among us, and this time we will embrace you. Save us from our sin, and you will never suffer again!

Create in us a clean heart, O God, and put a new and right spirit within us. Grant us the mind that was in Christ,[38] and we

---

34 See John 14:15-18; 8:32; I John 3:18-19.

35 See Matthew 11:16-19.

36 See Zephaniah 1:14-18.

37 See Isaiah 24:4-5.

38 See Philippians 2:5-6.

who have walked in darkness will behold a great light; we who have dwelled in a land of deep shadows, on us shall a light shine.[39] And your people shall say on that day, "Lo, this is the Lord for whom we have waited; let us rejoice in our salvation."[40]

That day can be *this* day, O Lord! So much we know, so little we trust! Give us the courage to turn about and return to you. Deliver us from our vanity, that we might give our gifts and pray our prayers not for recognition, but out of gratitude. Deliver us, that we might fast the fast that *you* desire: the fast that will loose the bonds of wickedness and let the oppressed go free; the fast that will break its bread with the hungry and offer its house to the homeless; the fast that will refuse to hide its face from any brother or sister in need.

O Lord, give us the courage to turn about and return to you, and we will return to our neighbor. Then shall your light break forth like the dawn,[41] your grace ascending like the rising sun, and your mercy, as its ray.

*Benediction.* Go now; make peace with your God in the secrecy of your heart, that you might make peace with your neighbor in the service of the world.

## First Sunday in Lent

*Lections*: Deuteronomy 26:1-11; Psalm 91:9-16; Romans 10:8b-13; Luke 4:1-13

*Call to Worship*
L:   O sisters of Christ, where do you live?
W:   We live in the fields ripe unto harvest.[42]
L:   O brothers of Christ, where do you dwell?
M:   We dwell in the barns filled with first fruits.
L:   O children of God, where is your home?
A:   Our home is where we offer our baskets—the table of blessing, the altar of God!

---

39  Inspired by Isaiah 9:2.
40  See Isaiah 25:9.
41  See Isaiah 58:6-9.
42  Inspired by John 4:35.

*Invocation.* O Savior, you promise that all who cling to you will be delivered, that all who call upon you will be heard. We have clung too long to this world, O God; now we turn and reach for you. Stretch out your hand, deliver us! We have called too often upon other gods; now we turn and cry to you. Hear our prayer, Lord, and rescue us!

*Litany*

L: Hear now the word of the Lord, all who enter these doors to worship;

P: We come to worship the Lord our God, whom we have made our refuge!

L: If you would dwell in this, my house, you must change your ways!

P: Speak to us, Lord, for we would be faithful!

L: If you no longer estrange the stranger, if you no longer forsake the forsaken;

P: If we turn, and be friend to the friendless; if we turn, and be home to the homeless;

L: If you no longer be true to untruth, but execute justice among one another;

P: If we turn, and amend our ways, no longer chasing other gods—

L: Then I will let you inhabit this place—

P: This house where your glory dwells!

L: Like living stones, you will *become* my house—

P: And Christ will be the sure foundation, and the world will be the walls!

L: Hear my word and amend your ways, for then you will find your habitation!

P: Then goodness and mercy will brighten our days;

L: And you shall dwell in the house of God—

P: We shall *be* the house of God—

A: For ever and for ever![43]

*Prayer for One Voice.* O God, in whose service we find our freedom, we call upon your name with gratitude for the past and with hope for the future. Words of faith are upon our lips;

---

43 Much of this litany was drawn from Jeremiah 7:1-7; also inspired by Psalm 26:8; I Peter 2:5; Psalm 23:6.

songs of faith are upon our hearts. The words tell of your righteousness; the songs rejoice in your salvation. For you are the God of our ancestors, of our mothers and fathers who went down into Egypt and were enslaved by the hand of Pharaoh; who cried out to you in the land of Goshen and were heard, for you saw their affliction, their toil, their oppression, and delivered them into a land of milk and honey.

And you are the God of our savior, our brother Jesus, who with his parents went down into Egypt and was saved from the hand of Herod; who cried out to you in the Garden of Gethsemane and was heard, for you saw his torment, his struggle, his sorrow, and brought him into the kingdom of bread and wine.

We are grateful, Lord; for as we retell the story of your righteousness, we participate in that saving history and make it our hope. And our need for that hope is no less than in the past. Temptation creeps into the midst of our salvation. Our parents, having been led into the wilderness by your hand, wandered for forty years, and were sorely tempted; indeed, while you communed with Moses on Mount Sinai, they created a golden calf and proclaimed it god. And our brother, having been led into the wilderness by your Spirit, was tempted for forty days; and when every temptation was ended, his adversary departed only *until a more opportune time.*

The voice of the tempter taunts us, even as it taunted Jesus: *If* you are children of God, turn the stones to bread, and your hunger shall be satisfied! *If* you are children of God, seize the glory of power, and the world shall be yours! *If* you are children of God, throw yourselves off the roof of the temple, and you shall not be hurt! The voice seduces us, Lord, sounding like yours. So we live and die, trying to turn stones into bread, turning what we want into what we need, and believing, if we get it, that *you* have made it possible. We live and die, climbing the mountain, looking for more power than we have, and believing, if we find it, that *you* have made it happen. We live and die, leaping off the rooftops of our religion, testing the angels of your will, and believing, if we are rescued, that *you* have made it so.

O Lord, how little we comprehend the profanity of trying to tempt you! How little we understand the blasphemy of courting you, as if you could be won or lost; the blasphemy of negotiating with you, as if you could be bought or sold; the blasphemy of examining you, as if you could be judged right or wrong.

O Lord, how we deceive ourselves, believing that you play favorites, forgetting that you are Lord of all; that just as you are the God of the one who cried "Father!" on the cross, you are the God of those who cried "Baal!" before the golden calf; and you are the God of us who cry "Lord, Lord!" and do not do your will.[44]

Forgive us, Lord, for we sin.

Forgive us, Lord, for we would overcome temptation.

Forgive us, Lord, for you alone would we serve—you, in whom alone we find freedom.

*Benediction*

L: O sisters of the tempted Christ, to whom will you turn, and serve in faith?

W: We will turn to the Bread of Life and all who faint from hunger!

L: O brothers of the tempted Christ, to whom will you turn, and serve in faith?

M: We will turn to the Prince of Peace and all who long for justice!

L: O disciples of the tempted Christ, to whom will you turn, and serve in faith?

A: We will turn to the Lord of Lords and all who search for truth!

## Second Sunday in Lent

*Lections*: Genesis 15:1-12, 17-18; Psalm 27; Philippians 3:17–4:1; Luke 13:31-35

*Call to Worship*

L: People of God, be gathered together!

P: Like a hen with her brood beneath her wings, God has brought us together!

---

44 See Luke 6:46.

L: People of God, await Christ's coming!
P: Blessed is the one who comes in the name of the Lord of heaven!

*Invocation.* O Lord, send your word into our midst. Let us, like Abram, receive it honestly, despite our fear, and respond to it faithfully, despite our trembling. Assure the peoples of your presence, and we will enlist our passion in your service; assure creation of your care, and we will commit our courage to your cause.

Send your word into our lives, O God. Let it dwell in our flesh, and we, like the disciples, will receive it honestly, despite our fear, and respond to it faithfully, despite our trembling.

*Litany*
L: Fear not, O children of Abram and Sarai, for I am your strength and shield:[45]
P: The armor that deflects hatred in the crusade for peace;
L: The coat that combats cold with the cloth of compassion;
P: The arm that screens the sun in the desire for relief;
L: The shoulder that braves the wind in the search for hope;
P: The eye that keeps vigil in the war against indifference;
L: The home that shelters the heart in the wilderness of grief;
P: The candle that gladdens the night with the promise of presence;
L: The song that unites the singers in the struggle for freedom;
P: The chalk that draws the line in the moment of decision;
L: The window that reveals deceit in the glass of truth;
P: The hand that pricks pride with the needle of humility;
L: The balm that heals injury in the name of mercy;
P: The faith that dares question the certainty of belief.
L: Fear not, O children of Abram and Sarai:
P: For the Lord our God is our strength and shield!

*Prayer for One Voice.* O God, in gracious love you promise to care for the creatures of earth; in steadfast love you keep your promise. But we, who so quickly embrace your covenant, just as quickly betray it; we, from whom you desire worship, too often offer only scorn. For making and then keeping your

---

45 See Psalm 28:7.

promise in the greatness of your mercy, we sing your praise, Lord; and for accepting and then spurning your covenant in the greatness of our sin, we ask your forgiveness.

The reality of sin rages furiously in our lives, but the word *sin* sits quietly, often reluctantly, on our lips. Our mouths rebel against its confession, against our shame. How little we understand, Lord, that the confession, once spoken, and the shame, once named, can free us from sin—from the power of that which we allow out of fear, honor out of folly, cover by our silence, and cloak with our indifference!

You have lit the refiner's fire, Lord;[46] now make glowing embers of our sin. Let the penitent word burn on our tongues, scorching our lips until they are compelled to speak. Let them speak—not that we might grovel in confession, but that we might grow in courage; not that we might take pleasure in humiliation, but that we might receive power in liberation; not that we might wallow in guilt, but that we might rise up in faith.

Forgive us, Lord, for we have sinned.

The word burns, Lord. Let our hearts flame with truth— truth about you, about ourselves, about our neighbors: the truth of how, redeemed by you, we can redeem one another; how, freed by you, we can free one another; how, empowered by you, we can empower one another.

Forgive us, Lord, for we have sinned.

The word burns, Lord. Let our spirits be filled with light— the very Light of the World, the light that shines without blinding, leads without wavering, and glows without ceasing.

Forgive us, Lord, for we have sinned.

The word burns, Lord. Let our bodies dazzle in their transfiguration[47]—in the glory of your in-dwelling, the radiance of your in-spiriting, the brilliance of your in-fleshing.

Forgive us, Lord, for we have sinned.

The word burns, Lord. Let our hands take up the candles of peace—candles whose flame cannot be doused; whose tapers cannot be consumed; whose tallow cannot be melted.

Forgive us, Lord, for we have sinned.

---

46 Inspired by Malachi 3:2; Matthew 3:10-12.

47 Inspired by Luke 9:29.

O God, we lift our candles, our lives, to yours. We who so often betray you, embrace you now. We who so often scorn you, worship you now. In the greatness of our sin, we have asked forgiveness. In the greatness of your mercy, you have received us.

*Benediction.* O God, unless you be the stronghold of our life, our worship is in vain. So lay your hand upon our hands and your spirit upon our spirits; let your vision be our vision, and your work, our work.

## *Third Sunday in Lent*

*Lections:* Isaiah 55:1-9; Psalm 63; I Corinthians 10:1-13; Luke 13:1-9

*Call to Worship*
L:  The heavens rise high above the earth, higher than any bird can soar;
P:  The east lies distant from the west, more distant than any wind can blow;
L:  But above the greatest height does God raise up our hearts,
P:  And beyond the farthest distance does God remove our sins!
L:  Let us bless the Lord with all our soul—
A:  Let all that is within us bless God's holy name!

*Invocation.* As in a dry and weary land where no water is, our souls have thirsted for you, O Lord. Now we have come into your sanctuary; the shadow of your power and glory envelops us.

If you are near, Lord, do not remain silent; do not hide from us. Incline your ear, and come to us; hear, that our souls may live. Make with us an everlasting covenant, and we shall dwell in the shadow of your wings and sing your praise today, tomorrow and forever.

*Litany*
L:  *I shout to you from the wilderness.* Do you not hear me?
P:  O Lord our God, here are your people!
L:  Let the wicked forsake their ways, and the unrighteous their thoughts.

P: Each speck of dust is made by your hand; help us to honor the earth that supports our journey, here in this and every place!

L: *I shout to you on my way to Jerusalem.* Do you not hear me?

P: O Christ our Lord, here are your people!

L: Straighten your backs and square your shoulders, for the day on which you are healed is holy!

P: Each moment of time is held in your hand; help us to honor the life that mends our wounds, now on this and every day!

L: *I shout to you among the multitudes.* Do you not hear me?

P: O Christ our Lord, here are your people!

L: Stretch out your arms to those most rejected, for God will not let them be tempted beyond their strength!

P: Each act of compassion is blessed by your hand; help us to honor the love that uplifts our neighbor, offered to one and every soul!

*Prayer for One Voice.* O God of mercy, we behold a fig tree, and it is without fruit. And we say, "Let us chop it down; why should it use up the ground?" But you say, "No, feed it, and it may live." We approach the tree, curious, cautious, unaware that you convert the ordinary into the extraordinary. And you allow us to come, well aware that we frequently reduce the extraordinary to the ordinary.

O God of grace, we behold a fig tree dying, and you are not content simply to study us while we study its fruitless branches. You *speak,* and your voice is reassuring, so reassuring that we do not run away but call out, "Here we are!" Yet what you say is at once terrible and wonderful. You reveal yourself to be the God of Abraham and Sarah, of Isaac and Rebecca, of Jacob and Rachel and Leah; the God of Moses and Miriam, of Mary and Joseph, and of Jesus the Christ. You reveal yourself to be the mighty Creator, the eternal beginning and endless end, the infinite sky and bottomless sea, whose life depends on nothing, but whose love gives life to everything.

O God of patience, we behold a fig tree dying, and we hear your voice speaking. We believe you are in our midst, but we are not relieved. Your presence is demanding. Who you are

67

asserts that the world cannot remain as it is, that it must become something new. But change does not come as easily as our protests. "Let the wicked forsake their way, and I will abundantly pardon," you shout. And we object, "What if we are tempted beyond our strength?" "I am faithful, and I will give you strength," you cry. Still we complain, "What if we are unable to endure? Why should the risk be ours?" Another time, Lord; another place. Another way, Lord; another face.

O God of love, we see, and hear, and protest, but your purpose will not be thwarted. Pry open our eyes with a barren fig tree; make us see what you see—the deliverance of your people from the threat of death. Unstop our ears with its rustling branches; make us hear what you hear—the cry of the world's oppressed. If your fig tree be barren, let it not be consumed. If its twigs be leafless, let them not be lifeless. Convert the barren into the fruit-bearing, that common people might become uncommon prophets, receivers of new life from you, givers of new life to the world.

*Benediction.* O God, in Christ you remind us that every place is your sanctuary, every moment your holy moment, every person your beloved. Let us, by our care for the earth, our respect for each moment, and our concern for your people, bear witness to the sublimity of your love and to the sanctity of our life.

## Fourth Sunday in Lent

*Lections*: Joshua 5:9-12; Psalm 32; II Corinthians 5:16-21; Luke 15:1-3, 11-32

*Call to Worship*

L:  O magnify the Lord with me; let us exalt God's name together!

P:  For when we judge ourselves unworthy to be called the children of God, the Lord looks upon us with compassion, and runs to embrace us while we are still far away.

L:  O magnify the Lord with me; let us exalt God's name together!

P:  For when we judge our neighbors unworthy to be called the children of God, the Lord looks upon them and weeps for joy, and makes a great feast while we stand at a distance.

L: O magnify the Lord with me; let us exalt God's name together!

P: For the humble shall be received with honor, and the haughty shall be humbled; every prodigal shall return with hope, and every elder shall rejoice with gladness!

*Invocation.* O Lord, receive the prayer of your prodigal children! In the folly of our freedom, we have demanded much and conceded little; we have aimed high and stooped low. Now, after long and lonely wandering, we return home, seeking shelter for our sleep, bread for our hunger, and water for our thirst.

Open your arms, Lord; do not send us away! For happy are they who take refuge in you—who call to you, and are answered; who search for you, and are found; who trust in you, and are delivered!

*Litany*

L: Who is this, who feasts with sinners?

W: This is the God who loves the world; who kindles the light that will not be extinguished, that all creation might be saved.[48]

M: This is the Christ who loves the peoples; who embodies the life that will not be conquered, that all creation might be saved.

W: This is the parent who loves the child; who fosters the dream that will not be denied, that all creation might be saved.

M: This is the child who loves the parent; who forges the trust that will not be broken, that all creation might be saved.

W: This is the brother who loves the sister; who frees the spirit that will not be bound, that all creation might be saved.

M: This is the sister who loves the brother; who opens the door that will not remain closed, that all creation might be saved.

---

48 Inspired by John 3:16-17.

W:  This is the lover who loves the beloved; who reveres the bond that will not be severed, that all creation might be saved.

M:  This is the friend who loves the forsaken; who extends the hand that will not be withheld, that all creation might be saved.

L:  O Lord, let us feast while Pharisees whisper! Let the sound of our singing drown the scribes' murmurs!

A:  It is well to make merry and be glad, for the one who was dead is alive; the one who was lost is found!

*Prayer for One Voice.* O Lord, in you our souls make their boast. You are the God who frees the captive, who bears for them the burdens too great, and breaks for them the yokes too heavy, and suffers for them the wounds too grave. You are the God who strengthens the weak, who supports them against winds too strong, and shores them up in struggles too grim, and sustains them down roads too long. You are the God who renews the faint, who swims for them the waters too deep, and leaps for them the hurdles too high, and lights for them the ways too dark.

Stretch out your hand, O Lord, and we will flee the place of our oppression to follow you through the wilderness. Feed us with quail from the sky and manna from heaven; draw water from the rock for our thirst. And it will come to pass that we will need the quail and manna no longer. We will partake of the fruit of the land, of the fruit of our labors, of the harvest reaped by the hands of your people.

Yes, in you, O Lord, our souls make their boast, for in you they will be freed! They bless you at all times, for in you they will be strengthened! They exalt your name together, for in you they will be renewed!

Stretch out your hand, O God, and a new Moses will appear among us as we toil, summoning us to follow. Let him feed us with loaves and fishes; let him turn water into wine for our thirst. And it will come to pass that we will need the loaves and fishes no longer. We will partake of the bread of the kingdom, of the bread of life, of the loaf offered up by the hands of the savior!

Yes, in you, O Christ, our souls make their boast, for in you they will be freed! They bless you at all times, for in you they will be strengthened! They exalt your name together, for in you they will be renewed!

Stretch out your hand, O God, and a new spirit will descend upon us as we wait, to send us into the world. Let her feed us with milk, and the milk will satisfy our hunger and our thirst. But it will come to pass that we will need milk no longer. We will partake of solid food, of the food of prophets, of the feast prepared by the hands of an angel![49]

Yes, in you, O Spirit, our souls make their boast, for in you they will be freed! They bless you at all times, for in you they will be strengthened! They exalt your name together, for in you they will be renewed!

*Benediction.* Look to God and be radiant; let your faces shine. For you who were lost have been brought home; go forth into the world. You who were dead have been raised; give life unto the world. Go with God, and find! Go with God, and live!

## Fifth Sunday in Lent

*Lections*: Isaiah 43:16-21; Psalm 126; Philippians 3:4b-14; John 12:1-8

*Call to Worship*

L: Remember not the former things,
P: Nor dwell on the things of old—
L: For the Lord is doing a new thing; do you not perceive it?
P: Let us press on to make God's goal our own,
L: Forgetting whatever lies behind,
P: Straining toward what lies ahead!
L: As it was in the beginning,
P: It is now, and ever shall be—
L: World without end!
P: Amen!
A: Amen![50]

---

49 Inspired by I Corinthians 3:2; Hebrews 5:12-14; Revelation 10:8-9.
50 Last five lines were taken from "Glory Be to the Father" (Lesser Doxology, 3rd–4th century).

*Invocation.* O Christ, take hold of us! If we have fallen to the ground, lift us up. If we have lost sight of the finish, point the way. Grasp our hands and pull us forward, seize our spirits and urge them on; show us the course, and we will press toward the goal, toward the prize of our high calling as your people.

*Litany*

L: Let the feet of Christ be anointed, and let the world be filled with the fragrance!

P: As Christ washed our feet with water and dried them with a towel, we shall anoint his feet with ointment and wipe them with our hair:[51]

L: We shall anoint the wanderers of earth, soothing the feet that know no rest;

P: And we shall anoint the pilgrims, blessing the feet that seek places of truth.

L: We shall anoint the refugees of earth, welcoming the feet that have no home;

P: And we shall anoint the adventurers, blessing the feet that blaze trails of hope.

L: We shall anoint the stragglers of earth, inspiring the feet that have no passion;

P: And we shall anoint the rebels, blessing the feet that walk miles for justice.

L: We shall anoint the fugitives of earth, consoling the feet that find no help;

P: And we shall anoint the messengers, blessing the feet that bear words of peace.

A: O let the feet of Christ be anointed, and let the world be filled with the fragrance!

*Prayer for One Voice.* O eternal God, how often we worship you and how little we understand you:

You, who makes the first to be last and the last to be first;

You, who frees the slave and enslaves the free;

You, who makes wealth to be poverty and poverty, wealth;

You, who chides the pious and feasts with the faithless;

---

51 Inspired by John 13:5.

You, who makes foe to be friend and friend to be foe;
You, who brings the outsider in and turns the insider out;
You, who makes success to be failure and failure, success—
*You* are the God who calls us—a right-side-up people—to become your upside-down kingdom. You call us to be embodiments of a revolution in values, a revolution in which the power of love deposes the glory of our ambition, in which the freedom of grace breaks our bondage to greed. How you would love us, how you would save us—by changing us, by changing our world!

We must ask your forgiveness, Lord. For though you desire our conversion to a different world, we would rather preserve the world as it is. Though you desire us to defend the least among us, we would rather admire the greatest. Though you desire us to serve you faithfully at all times and in all places, we would rather confine our faith to the services in our sanctuaries. Though you desire us to become your upside-down people, we would rather climb the ladder of right-side-up living.

If only we could say with Paul that we count all gain as loss for your sake.[52] If only we could offer all that we have, and all that we are, in the service of all that you would have us become. If only we could realize that to be baptized is to be turned around, transformed, transfigured; to be made a new creature, with new eyes to see rightly, new ears to hear wisely, new lips to speak truly, new minds to think clearly, new hearts to love greatly; to begin to discern what *right* and *wise* and *true* and *clear* and *great* might mean, in the life of radical faith.

If only!

We confess our difficulty in discerning your values, Lord. When your revelation comes, it is neither easily perceived nor wholeheartedly received. Even when Christ appears, revealing your values in body and soul, we cannot agree upon his identity. We hesitate to recognize him, refuse to acknowledge him: His words are too harsh, his ways are too hard. He is one of us, yet so unlike us; he offends and confronts, he disrupts and disputes, he defies and demands, and he loves—Great God, how he loves!

---

52 See Philippians 3:7.

Such scandal, this love for sinners! Such shame, this love for enemies! Such disgrace, this love for outcasts!

If only!

O Lord, stand our values on their head, if they are not also your values. We are capable of becoming upside-down for your sake, but we are not strong. Send your spirit into our very bones, into the sinew of our flesh, into the substance of our souls; make us burn with the fire of compassion, with the flame of conviction, with the light of zeal!

Then we shall understand you whom we worship, and we shall begin to be what we have begun to understand:

We will make first to be last and last to be first;

We will free the slave and enslave the free;

We will make wealth to be poverty and poverty, wealth;

We will chide the pious and feast with the faithless;

We will make foe to be friend and friend to be foe;

We will bring the outsider in and turn the insider out;

We will make success to be failure and failure, success—

We will be your upside-down people, the embodiments of your revolution in values. And, oh, how we will love you! How we will serve you—by changing ourselves, by changing our world!

*Benediction.* May the Lord make a way for you through the wilderness and bring you together into the promised land, that your mouth might be filled with laughter, and your tongue with shouts of joy!

## Passion/Palm Sunday

*Lections:* Isaiah 50:4-9*a*; Psalm 31:9-16; Psalm 118:19-29; Philippians 2:5-11; Luke 19:28-40; Luke 22:14–23:56

*Call to Worship*

L: This morning God shall awaken our ears to hear, as those who were taught by Christ,

P: And we shall console the forlorn through the dignity of our hearing.

L: This morning God shall awaken our eyes to see, as those who were taught by Christ,

P:  And we shall inspire the tired through the integrity of our seeing.
L:  This morning God shall awaken our tongues to speak, as those who were taught by Christ,
P:  And we shall sustain the weary through the authority of our speaking.
A:  O, this is the day that the Lord has made; let us rejoice and be glad in it!

*Invocation.* O God, your messiah draws near. We have cut the palm branches, we have spread our coats over the muddy road, all to welcome his coming. Shall we praise you for all the mighty works that we have seen? Shall we shout *Hosanna!* with the crowd?

We want a messiah, but is this the messiah we want? Confront us with the moment of decision, O Lord. And if we remain speechless as he passes by, if we stand by the road in timid silence, let the very stones beneath our feet cry out, saying, "Blessed is the one who comes in the name of the Lord!"

*Litany*

L:  He comes to you on a colt never ridden, and his face is set before you like flint.
P:  O God, you are our help! Tell us: Who is this carpenter-king whom we hail? What is this day that has swept us away?
L:  Do you not recognize the Bethlehem baby, who arrived to the singing of anthems and slept in the silence of awe?
P:  The baby who inspired the joy of the angels and kindled the hope of the peoples? Glory to you in the highest, and peace to all on earth![53]
L:  Do you not recognize the temple youth, who questioned the answers of sages and answered the questions of teachers?
P:  The youth who amazed the minds of the elders and astonished the hearts of his parents? Glory to you in the highest, and peace to all on earth!

---

53 See Luke 2:14; 19:38.

L:   And do you not recognize the Nazareth prophet, who proclaimed release to the captives and demanded relief for the poor?

P:   The prophet who preached salvation for our foes and was thrown out of our city?[54] Who is *he* to be glorified? How can *he* be the Chosen One?[55]

L:   And do you not recognize the Jewish messiah, who was anointed king by a woman's hand, who established the kingdom for servants and sinners?

P:   The messiah who sleeps in the house of outcasts and feasts at the table of fools? Who is *he* to be glorified? How can *he* be the Chosen One? O God, tell us: How can we hail this carpenter-king or honor this day that has swept us away?

L:   He comes to you on a colt that none has ever ridden. Tell me: How soon will you take him to the tomb where none has ever lain?

*Prayer for One Voice.* O God, your servant—our Christ—comes among us this day, and we join the multitudes who celebrate his coming. We adorn his head with the crown of our hope, we cloak his shoulders with the robe of our joy. He sits astride a colt never ridden, but it is the power of our expectations that really carries him into our midst. He knows our expectations better than we; they taunt him with a seductive voice, tempting him to be someone you have not meant him to be, someone you have not sent him to be.

O Lord, little do we understand that, in the space of a week, our songs of praise will turn into shouts of ridicule; or that we will replace the crown of hope with one of thorns, and the robe of joy with one of mockery. Little do we understand that, in the space of a week, this Jesus will fall from glory to shame; that his eye will waste from grief, and his life be spent with sorrow; that his strength will fail because of his misery, and his bones will waste away. Why must he become the scorn of his enemies, a horror to his neighbors, an object of dread to his friends?

---

54  See Luke 4.

55  Inspired by Luke 23:35.

Why must he listen to our whispers as we scheme together against him, as we plot to take his life, until he is made a broken jar, crushed in the dirt beneath our heel?

Why, Lord? We understand little, for we do not understand ourselves. You sent this God-man to serve us, to save us, that we might learn to serve others, to save others. But, caught up in mighty dreams and changing times, we have not served even *him*. Instead, we have sought to control him, disciples rising above their teacher. Forgive us, Lord, for while we have stood waving our palm branches, we have wondered how supporting him might be to our benefit, how using him might be to our advantage. Forgive us, for when he has spoken, we have listened for the right words, the easy words, words we have wanted him to speak; and when he has acted, we have watched for the right deeds, easy deeds, deeds we have wanted him to do. Can we, who have not genuinely served him, really be expected to save him?

O God, hear our confession: More than any change for which we yearn, we need a change in mind. Inspire in us the mind that is in Christ, who humbles himself and is obedient, who will be faithful to your will even unto death, even unto death on a hateful cross. If we are too proud to follow him, cast out our vanity, and let us become modest disciples. If we are too angry to follow him, dispel our hostility, and let us become makers of peace. If we are too hesitant to follow him, exorcise our fear, and let us become bearers of courage. Help us to follow him as faithfully as he has followed you, Lord, and we will serve others as he has served us; we will save others, as he has saved us, and we will rescue his life from the traps we ourselves have laid.

*Benediction.* Let us have the mind among ourselves that is ours because it was Christ's. And let us go and do for our neighbor as Christ has done for us.

## Holy Thursday

*Lections:* Exodus 12:1-4 (5-10), 11-14; Psalm 116:1-2, 12-19; I Corinthians 11:23-26; John 13:1-17, 31b-35

## LITANIES AND OTHER PRAYERS

*Call to Worship*

L:  Let us draw near to the presence of God;
P:  Let us call on the name of the Lord!
L:  For the day draws near when we shall behold the savior,
P:  When each heart that has been broken by the strong arm of sin shall be bound up and healed by the hand of salvation!

*Invocation.* O Teacher, we have walked a long road with you. We have watched you: a baby, adored by shepherds from the fields; a youth, questioned by teachers in the temple; a man, plunged into the waters of baptism; the Son, led into the wilderness of temptation; the Servant of the Lord, rejected by the people of Nazareth; the Chosen One, transfigured in the company of prophets; the *Christ of God*—speaking the unspeakable and doing the unthinkable, calling the unworthy and cleansing the unclean, healing the unwell, and forgiving the unforgivable.

From Bethlehem to Jerusalem, from a lowly stable to the upper room, we have followed you, watching you love the unloved. On this, the greatness of your love, we set our hope— we, who have so loved the world that we shall give you up to save ourselves.[56]

*Litany*

L:  The hour has come; our teacher awaits.
P:  The meal is prepared; the table is spread.
L:  Grasp the cup!
P:  Shall we lift the wine unto the Lord, or raise it to the world?
L:  "Take and drink; share its power until the reign of God has come on earth."
P:  O Christ, let this be a cup of blessing,[57] and not a cup of wrath!
L:  Break the bread!
P:  Shall we lift the loaf unto the Lord, or raise it to the world?
L:  "Take and eat; share its power until the reign of God has come on earth."

---

56  In contrast with John 3:16-17.
57  See I Corinthians 10:16.

P: O Christ, let it be the bread of life, and not the bread of mourning![58]

L: Are we able to drink what Christ must drink? Are we able to eat what Christ must eat?

P: Lord, we are able!

A: Let us pour out the cup of salvation, that all who thirst might be satisfied! Let us share the bread of redemption, that all who hunger might be filled!

*Prayer for One Voice.* O God, this Last Supper awakens memories of a Passover when, instead of a man, there was a boy; instead of a teacher among disciples in an upper room, there was a youth among teachers in the temple; instead of a lifted cup and a broken loaf, there was a question risked and an answer dared; instead of a haughty boast from his companions, there was only an air of wonder.

How far Jesus has journeyed between these Passovers! And how far we have walked with him, O God, not to understand! But this night, the hour has come. We sit at table, and Jesus takes a cup, saying, "Take this, and divide it among yourselves." And he takes the bread and breaks it, and gives it to us, saying, "This is my body; do this in remembrance of me." We listen and we watch, but we do not understand. We pass the cup with trembling hands; we pass the bread with lowered eyes.

Lord, we remember the mountain where he taught us, saying, "Blessed are those who hunger and thirst for righteousness, for they shall be satisfied." Satisfied—as the wedding party was satisfied by water turned to wine, as the five thousand were satisfied by a few loaves and fishes.[59] We remember, but we do not understand.

Receive the cup and the loaf *in remembrance,* he says. But what is about to happen, O God, that he should become a mere memory? What is yet to come, that his body should be broken and his blood spilled? What is this *new covenant* of which he speaks? What is this *new and living way* he opens?

---

58  See John 6:35; Jeremiah 16:7; Matthew 20:22.
59  See Matthew 5:1-2, 6; John 2:1-11; Luke 9:12-17.

O Lord, enliven our souls that we might follow his way, enlighten our minds that we might understand his truth, and empower our spirits that we might embody his life. For the *way* of the cup and the loaf is within us; you have written it upon our hearts. And the *truth* of the cup and the loaf is that you shall be our God, and we shall be your people. And the *life* of the cup and the loaf is knowing you—*all* of us knowing you, from the least of us to the greatest.

Make our hearts burn within us,[60] O God. In our communion, transform us; make us a parable of the kingdom and a sign unto the world. If we are caught up in the rapture of our pride, humble us, lest we miss our calling. For Christ anoints us as he was anointed: to preach good news to the poor, to proclaim release to the captives and recovering of sight to the blind, to set at liberty those who are oppressed and to proclaim the acceptable year of the Lord.[61] Upon *us* Christ confers the mission and the power that we had thought was his alone.

By your love you can save the sinful and make them a sign, O Lord. But if we think our hunger and thirst be already satisfied, Christ's way is not yet our way; his truth is not yet our truth; his life is not yet our life. Though we lift the cup and break the bread with him tonight, tomorrow he shall die alone. We shall forsake him, for we have not yet read what your finger has written upon our hearts.

Forgive us, Lord, for we thought we knew you; forgive us, for we do not know ourselves.

*Benediction.* The Lord prepared a table for Christ in the presence of his enemies.[62] Yet, when Christ lifted the cup, it overflowed; when Christ broke the bread, it multiplied. So let us hold fast to our hope. For even as we remember the mercy of the Lord, the Lord will forgive our iniquity and remember our sin no more.

---

60  See Luke 24:32.

61  Inspired by Luke 4:18-20.

62  Inspired by Psalm 23:5.

LENTEN SEASON

## Good Friday

*Lections*: Isaiah 52:13–53:12; Psalm 22; Hebrews 4:14-16; 5:7-9; John 18–19

*Call to Worship*

L: Listen. Do you hear the voice of the Lord?
P: For this we were born, to hearken unto heaven!
L: Be still. Do you hear that whispered word?
P: For this we came into the world, to bear witness to the truth!
L: What is this truth, that you should proclaim it?
P: The truth is flesh and walks among us, a shepherd who saves the sheep!

*Invocation.* O Christ, our Christ, why have we forsaken you? Why are we so far from you, so deaf to the sounds of your groaning? You appeal to us, but are not saved; you trust us, but are not requited. We despise and reject you; we hide our eyes from the sight of you. We mock and scoff at you; we wag our heads, taunting, "You trust the Lord; let the Lord deliver you!"

We pronounce sentence upon you, yet you remain silent. We tempt you to save yourself, but you resist temptation. We shout that we desire no ruler but Caesar, and you are nailed to a cross that proclaims you king.

O Lord, our Lord, do not forsake us, even though we have forsaken you and gone astray!

*Litany*

L: They seek him in the garden, and he steps from the shadows of the trees into the light of the moon, saying,
P: "I am the one."
L: "Who are you that you should declare, '*I* am the one'?"
P: "I am the good shepherd.[63] *Your* shepherds have led you astray, turning you away from good pastures. From mountain to hill you have wandered; you have forgotten your fold, but I will bring you home."
L: "Who are you that you should declare, '*I* am the one'?"

---

63 See John 10:11.

81

P: "You have been scattered over the face of the earth, with none to seek or search for you. So I myself have searched; I myself have sought you. And I will rescue you, and lead you to green pastures."

L: "Who are you that you should declare, 'I am the one'?"

P: "I am the one who will find the lost; I will bring back the strayed, and bind up the crippled; I will strengthen the weak, and feed you on justice."[64]

L: They recognize you outside the court, and you slip from the light of the moon into the shadows of the walls. They pursue you, saying, "Are not you among his disciples?"

P: "We are not the ones!"

L: "Who are you that you should declare, 'We are not the ones'? Which of you has not strayed from the ninety-and-nine, to be found by him with great rejoicing?"[65]

P: "We are not the ones!"

L: "Which of you, knowing the sound of his voice, did not hear and follow when he called you by name?"[66]

P: "We are not the ones!"

L: Then, behold, he shall lay down his life for you like a sheep in the midst of wolves. Weep, O people, for the one who knows you has come, and you have turned away![67]

*Prayer for One Voice.* O Christ, our Good Shepherd, how fitting that your birth was first announced to shepherds abiding in the fields! Shepherds who hurried to Bethlehem to find you lying in a manger! Shepherds who glorified and praised God for all they had heard and seen! And how fitting that your mother watched silently, pondering in her heart![68]

Where are the shepherds today, Lord, while your mother's heart is crucified at the foot of your cross?

O Christ, our Wise One, how fitting that your cradle was sought by magi from the East! Magi who followed your star across the sky! Magi who rejoiced and fell down before you,

---

64 Inspired by Jeremiah 50:6-7; Ezekiel 34.
65 Inspired by Matthew 18:10-14.
66 See John 10:1-18.
67 Inspired by Matthew 10:16; John 10:17; Luke 19:44b.
68 See Luke 2:8-20.

offering their gifts![69] And how fitting that your mother watched silently, wondering in her heart!

Where are the magi today, Lord, while your mother's heart is broken as your robe is gambled away?

O Christ, our Good Teacher, how fitting that you sought the company of teachers, even in your youth! Teachers who sat with you in the temple! Teachers who were amazed at your understanding and astonished by your answers! And how fitting that your mother watched silently, meditating in her heart!

Where are the teachers today, Lord, while your mother's heart is pierced, even as your side?

Where, indeed, are we, O Lord? We who in Nazareth heard you state your mission! We who spoke so well of you, marveling at your gracious words! We who saw you heal the paralytic and were filled with awe! We who witnessed your stilling of the angry winds and waves and were overwhelmed, whispering among ourselves![70] Where, indeed, are we?

We who in Jerusalem reveled in your coming, spreading our garments on the road before you—how we blessed you! We who sat at your table in the upper room, breaking the bread and swearing our devotion—how we loved you! We who stood by your side in the garden, brandishing our swords against your enemies—how we would have fought for you!

Where, indeed, are we now, O Lord? Now that you, the Good Shepherd, have become the lamb; now that you, the Wise One, have made foolish the wisdom of the world;[71] now that you, the Good Teacher, have taught the lesson we did not want to learn?

Where are we, indeed, while you deliver your beloved mother and your beloved friend into each other's care?

*Benediction.* O Christ, who shouldered the cross though you prayed to be spared the cup, grant us the grace to shoulder *our* cross, that the cup might pass from others.

---

69  See Matthew 2:1-12.

70  See Luke 4:16-30; 5:17-26; 8:22-26.

71  See I Corinthians 1:20.

# Easter Season

## Easter

*Lections:* Acts 10:34-43; Isaiah 65:17-25 (alternate); Psalm 118:1-2, 14-24; I Corinthians 15:19-26; Acts 10:34-43 (alternate); John 20:1-18; Luke 24:1-12 (alternate)

*Call to Worship*
L:  The baby was born in a stable;
P:  Today he arose from the grave!
L:  The child was wrapped in swaddling clothes;
P:  Today his shroud lies empty!
L:  Behold the new heavens, the angels singing;
P:  Behold the new earth, the stone rolled away!

*Invocation.* O Lord, this is your doing: Christ had passed through the gates of death, but today you have brought him through the gates of life. Now, triumphant, you open the marvelous gates even unto us, who nailed the Messiah to the tree.

O let the gates swing wide, that all might enter with thanksgiving! For in your city we shall behold no temple but you, and no shrine but the Christ; we shall see no sun but your glory, and no lamp but the Lamb. By this light shall we walk, coming into your presence with songs of praise.[72]

*Litany*
L:  Woman, why are you weeping? Who is the one you seek?
W:  They've carried away the body of my Lord, and nobody knows where they've laid him!
M:  O Mary, don't you weep, don't you mourn! O Mary, don't you weep!
L:  Why do you seek the living here among the dead?
W:  How can this be, this miracle I've seen? I'll run to tell the others, but who will dare believe?

---

72  Inspired by Revelation 21:22-26; 22:14.

M:   O Mary, don't you weep, don't you mourn! O Mary, don't you weep!

L:   Have they forgotten what he said, that he would rise again?

W:   Yes, they think I tell an idle tale; I show them the cloths, but they sit and wonder.

M:   O Mary, don't you weep, don't you mourn! O Mary, don't you weep!

L:   Do they not know that none shall die, that all will live forever?

W:   They stay at home, they close their shutters; the Teacher's message goes unheeded, it falls on deafened ears.

M:   O Mary, don't you weep, don't you mourn! O Mary, don't you weep! 'Cause when you get to heaven you're going to sing and shout; nobody there is going to turn you out! O Mary, don't you weep![73]

*Prayer for One Voice.* O God, who hears our call before our lips move, who answers our call before it is raised, we praise you for being present among us, for being present *to* us. We praise you especially for being present among us in Jesus Christ, whose life has revealed to us who you are and who we can aspire to become. His life has been truly yours, even while succumbing to the forces of death. And this day he has risen in your glory; he has revealed himself to the women, to those who stayed with him until his terrible end on the cross, and these women have spread the good news: This Christ is the living Lord of all, even of us, who denied knowing him; and you, O God, are the living God of all, even of us, who crucified him.

This grace of yours, O God—how hard it is to understand, how hard it is to accept! We have mocked the weak and admired the mighty, yet you have loved us—you, who honor the meek and humble the strong. We have abandoned the powerless and tolerated the pitiless, yet you have embraced us—you, who sustain the helpless and subvert the ruthless. Why, O God?

---

73  Based on the African-American spiritual "O Mary, Don't You Weep."

Christ taught us to turn the cheek, and instead we turned away from him. Why have you not turned from us? Christ urged us to call upon your name, and instead we called out for Barabbas. Why have you not called down a curse upon our heads? Christ chose us to proclaim your kingdom, and instead we proclaimed, "We've no king but Caesar!" Why have you not proclaimed, "Enough! No more! You are not my people, and I am not your God"?

We do not understand; the mystery of your grace is too great, too wonderful, too scandalous. But we *accept* this gospel, this good news, this resurrection—a resurrection not only of the Christ, but of us. *We are become his body!* The stone is rolled away! Unwrap the shroud that confines us, O God, and we shall walk out of this place of death; ours shall be a new life, and we shall walk upon a different earth and under a different sky, where former things are not remembered. Now, if any member of this body suffers, all of us shall suffer together; and if any member of this body rejoices, all of us shall rejoice together.[74]

Christ has risen—we are his body—and all the world rises with us! Glory to you, O God, our savior! Glory to you, for you have hearkened to our unspoken cry and become our salvation, that we might save the world! Glory to you, for the sound of weeping will no more be heard, and the call of distress will no more be raised! The tomb is empty! Grace has triumphed over the grave, and love is alive! O God, *love us into loving* more and better, that we—the risen body—might bear all things, and believe all things, and hope all things, and endure all things—all of us together![75]

*Benediction.* Disciples, do not take the good news of Easter to be an idle tale. That which is broken shall be whole again! That which has died shall live again! Believe in the gospel, and rise up in power! The wolf and the lamb shall feed together, and the lion shall eat straw like the ox; none shall hurt or destroy on all the Lord's mountain, and the reign of God shall come!

---

74  Inspired by I Corinthians 12:26.
75  Inspired by I Corinthians 13:7.

## Second Sunday of Easter

*Lections:* Acts 5:27-32; Psalm 118:14-29; Revelation 1:4*b*-8; John 20:19-31

*Call to Worship*

L: I welcome you! In the name of the One who was and is and ever shall be, I greet you!

P: Grace be with you! Grace to the world from the Genesis People, the image of God, a fruitful garden!

L: I embrace you! In the name of the One who lived and died and rose again, I receive you!

P: Peace be with you! Peace to the world from the Easter People, the body of Christ, a new creation!

*Invocation.* The rulers conspire upon their thrones, the peoples plot within their dwellings—even the disciples scheme behind closed doors, wondering, "How can we save ourselves?"

But the one who sits in the heavens laughs!

Laugh, O God! Pity us for pitting our power against yours, even as Pilate and the priests pitted their power against Jesus. Pity us for putting our desires above yours, even as the crowds and the disciples put their desires above Jesus. Yes, laugh, O God, and turn the folly of sinners into the fidelity of saints, even as you turned the tragedy of the crucifixion into the triumph of the resurrection!

*Litany*

L: Are you apostles of the one called Christ?

P: Our hands have touched the holes in his palms, our eyes have seen the wound in his side; we have known suffering, and received his peace: We are apostles of the one called Christ.

L: We commanded you not to teach in his name, yet you fill the world with the sound of your teaching.

P: The spirit of Easter has anointed our lips. We must obey God, not human beings.

L: We commanded you not to heal in his name, yet you fill the world with the joy of your healing.

P: The spirit of Easter has anointed our hands. We must obey God, not human beings.

L: We commanded you not to make peace in his name, yet you fill the world with the peace you have made.

P: The spirit of Easter has anointed our minds. We must obey God, not human beings.

L: We commanded you not to do good in his name, yet you fill the world with the good you have wrought.

P: The spirit of Easter has anointed our will. We must obey God, not human beings.

L: So, apostles, shall you defy us? Shall you resist your highest leaders?

P: The spirit of Easter has fallen upon us, to preach good news to the poor and proclaim release to the captives! We have seen, and we believe. May the Lord God help your *unbelief!*[76]

*Prayer for One Voice.* O God, Alpha and Omega, who in Jesus Christ turns the world upside-down, who makes folly of the world's wisdom and wisdom of the world's folly, who mocks the strength of the strong and crowns the weakness of the humble, you are our sovereign and savior, and we adore you.

We thank you, O Lord, for Easter: for the ways it kindles our awareness of who Jesus was and what he was about; of who you are and what you are about; of who we are and what we are about. In Jesus your character and our destiny were joined, and you promised that his work would not end with his death. You kept that promise, dear Lord; not only did the apostles take you at your word, they took your word to the world. And for this we thank you: not only for the favor with which the world responded to them, but for the faith with which they confronted the world.

When we compare our faith with theirs, O God, we are humbled. They were bold; we are timid. They turned the crucifixion into a model for discipleship; we turn discipleship into an alternative to crucifixion. They interpreted Easter as a summons to choose between divine and human rule; we inter-

---

76 Inspired by Luke 4:18.

pret Easter as the divine sanction of human rule. They received the resurrection as a call for radical decision; we receive it as a proof of ultimate security. They identified the suffering servant with the risen Lord; we glorify the risen Lord at the expense of the suffering servant.

Forgive us, O God, for separating Good Friday from Easter: for believing that, because our Lord's Easter lay behind us, no Golgotha lies before us; for supposing that, because he risked everything, we need not risk anything. Forgive us, above all, for thinking that, because we praise him loudly, we need not follow him closely.

We acknowledge, O God, that our divorce of Easter from Good Friday has done us no good and others much harm. Help us to proclaim the oneness of the empty tomb and the cross, to narrow the gap between our confession and our conduct. Empower us so to live that our works will confirm the words of our Lord about true greatness. Send us into the world, as you sent him into the world, to become the victorious servants of all.

*Benediction.* As God sent Christ to us, so now Christ sends us to the world. Let us not be faithless. Let us not lock ourselves in the upper room. But let us go down into the streets and do as he asks, allowing his grace to overpower our doubt and his peace to overcome our fear.

## Third Sunday of Easter

*Lections:* Acts 9:1-20; Psalm 30; Revelation 5:11-14; John 21:1-19

*Call to Worship*

L:  Join me on the Way, and our eyes shall see a heavenly light.
P:  Lead us up the higher road, even if the light should blind us.
L:  Join me on the Way, and our ears shall hear a heavenly voice.
P:  Lead us up the higher road, even if the voice should deafen us.

L: Join me on the Way, and our lives shall gain a heavenly cause.

P: Lead us up the higher road, even if the cause should test us.

A: We're marching to Zion, beautiful, beautiful Zion; we're marching upward to Zion, the beautiful city of God![77]

*Invocation.* O Lord, appear to us in a vision, though the glory of your face should make us shield our eyes. Speak to us a revelation, though the power of your voice should make us cover our ears.

We do not know who you are. We do not know what we do. O God, if you would make us your chosen instruments, if you would have us be faithful disciples, blind us, that we might see you more clearly; deafen us, that we might hear you more truly. Then we will know more fully whose we are and who we can become.

*Litany*

L: Worthy is the Lamb who was slain!

P: Let our lives be worthy of the Lamb's power; may the Lord use our weakness to shame the strong.[78]

L: Worthy is the Lamb who was slain!

P: Let our lives be worthy of the Lamb's wealth; may the Lord use our poverty to shame the greedy.

L: Worthy is the Lamb who was slain!

P: Let our lives be worthy of the Lamb's wisdom; may the Lord use our folly to shame the shrewd.

L: Worthy is the Lamb who was slain!

P: Let our lives be worthy of the Lamb's might; may the Lord use our frailty to shame the great.

L: Worthy is the Lamb who was slain!

P: Let our lives be worthy of the Lamb's honor; may the Lord use our lowliness to shame the lofty.

L: Worthy is the Lamb who was slain!

---

77 From Isaac Watts and Robert Lowry, "Marching to Zion."
78 See I Corinthians 1:27.

P: Let our lives be worthy of the Lamb's glory; may the Lord use our humility to shame the exalted.[79]

L: Worthy is the Lamb who was slain!

P: May all power and wealth and wisdom and might and honor and glory be unto the Lamb of God, forever and forever!

*Prayer for One Voice.* O Christ, we had thought you dead: We mourned in hiding, grieving your death and lamenting our loss, fearing a future without you. When finally we emerged from our hiding places, we hurried back to our old routines, our old priorities, our old livelihoods. We were determined to put the past behind us, to forget it like a bad dream. We sacrificed your visions to common sense; we surrendered our ideals to the "real" world. But our labors were empty—until we caught a glimpse of you on the shore, until you instructed us to cast our net on the other side of the boat.

You are our brother, Lord—our brother, our master, our teacher, our friend, you are all these things and more. But, though we spring into the sea and swim to the shore and run to greet you on the beach, you are not convinced of our love. Who would not adore you when their nets are full of fish?

Three times you ask us, "Disciples, do you love me?" Three times we insist, "Lord, you know that we do!" And you can only reply, "Then feed my lambs, and tend my sheep; feed my flock, and follow me."

O risen brother, who breaks bread with us like no one we have ever known, we confess that our love for you has been timid. We have been faithful to you in the good times and faithless in the bad. When we believed you to be dead and buried, the fire died in our souls, and we buried our hopes in a tomb that was deeper and darker than yours, a tomb carved out by our fears. But now your return has rolled the stone away, and all our confidence and conviction and courage stride out into the sunlight, resurrected by the sound of your voice.

We behold you, O Christ, and in the radiance of your presence, we behold how absent has been our faith. Forgive us. We

79 Inspired by I Corinthians 1:28-29.

have let living take precedence over loving; we have let self hold sway over neighbor. So you must remind us that the only measure of our regard for the shepherd is our regard for the flock. "If you love me," you repeat, "feed my lambs, tend my sheep, feed my flock, follow me."

O Christ, once you called us to be fishers; now you summon us also to be shepherds. Help us to watch over the flock that you have entrusted to our care—not grudgingly, not because we have to do so, but willingly, because we want to do so.[80] Once you called us to be disciples; now you summon us also to be servants. Help us to serve the ones you have placed in our path—the hungry and the thirsty, the naked and the stranger, the sick and the imprisoned. Help us to open our arms to those we once despised or ignored, to those we once persecuted by what we did or did not do. Help us to bless them, saying, "Come, inherit the kingdom prepared for you from the foundation of the world."[81]

O Lord, we have proclaimed with our lips that you are the Son of God; help us to proclaim with our lives that we are the people of God. With our words we have confessed our love for you; help us, with our deeds, to confess your love for the world.

*Benediction.* Receive now the blessed promise of Easter: Every night shall be broken by dawn, and every tear shall spring from joy; every step shall become a dance, and every word shall carry a song.

This promise is yours to share. Carry it to those still standing on Golgotha; take it to those still trapped on Good Friday. Let your souls erupt in praise—let them not be silent!

## Fourth Sunday of Easter

*Lections:* Acts 9:36-43; Psalm 23; Revelation 7:9-17; John 10:22-30

---

80  See I Peter 5:2.

81  Inspired by Matthew 25:34-35.

*Call to Worship*
L: Witnesses, gather! Embrace the word of the world's salvation!
P: We have washed our robes; they gleam in the sun. Now we come before the Lord!
L: Witnesses, gather! Embody the word for the world's salvation!
P: We shall wipe every tear from the world's eyes, and all shall dwell with the Lord forever!
A: Salvation belongs to the Lord our God! Salvation belongs to the Lord!

*Invocation.* O Lord, you were the shepherd of the Lamb; he did not go astray. The rabbis tempted him to tarry in the temple, but he obeyed the command of his parents to return home. Satan baited him with promises of great power and authority, but he listened, instead, to your still small voice. His disciples encouraged him to answer hate with rage, but he turned aside and went another way. He prayed to be spared the cup of agony, but he ended up doing not his will but yours.

O Lord, you sent the Lamb to be our shepherd; we shall not go astray. let us hear his voice, and follow him all the days of our lives, that we may do not our will but yours.

*Litany*
L: O world, what has come to you this day, that you should fall on your knees and worship?
P: *Salvation!*
L: You have cried an ocean of tears; how can you say that your suffering shall end?
P: Salvation *belongs to God!*
L: Perhaps for a day, your hunger can be filled; perhaps for a week, your thirst can be slaked—
P: Salvation belongs to God *forever!*
L: Maybe today your tears shall cease, but what will flow from your eyes tomorrow?
P: Salvation belongs to God, *forever and forever!*
L: But what of glory and wisdom and honor and might? Are they not within your reach?

P: Salvation belongs to God, forever and forever, *amen!*

L: Then, world, put your hand in the hand of the Lord! Nothing can snatch you from the Lord's grasp!

P: *Salvation belongs to the Lord our God, forever and forever, amen!*

*Prayer for One Voice.* O Creator God, Breath of the universe and Heartbeat of the earth, you are our beginning and our end and our in-between. You are our salvation—not only on this, but on every day. You are our deliverance—not only for ourselves, but for our neighbor. You are our redemption—not only from our sin, but from those who sin against us.

O God, we need you. We are frail, but your strength makes us strong in our frailty. We are foolish, but your wisdom makes us wise in our folly. We are vain, but your humility makes us humble in our vanity. Your life in us makes us more and better than we are. For this we praise you: not that you stoop to us, but that you lift us up; not that you condescend to care for us, but that you elevate us to care for one another.

This is your way, Lord. This is your truth. And in Christ we see that this is your life. His works, done in your name, bear witness to you. Yet, though we assent to what he says and admire what he does, we do not believe with all our heart and soul and mind and strength. Time and again, we beg for reassurance: "If this one is really the Christ," we say, "tell us plainly." Time and time again, we plead for another sign: "If this one is truly the Christ, show us clearly."

O Lord, forgive us for our disbelief in the presence of such a divine life—of such a human life—as that of Jesus Christ. Understand the greatness of our temptation to opt out of your way, to opt for another truth, to opt into another life. As time passes, the glory of the open grave pales; more and more we remember the shame, the pain of the rugged cross. Our once-certain step falters; our once-constant faith wavers. Can we really drink of the cup? Are we really willing to receive the baptism that was Christ's?[82] Can we really carry our cross? Are we really willing to carry our neighbor's?

---

82  See Mark 10:38-39.

Our temptation is to find another Christ to follow. Though this Christ be yours, though this Christ be risen, we would make him someone else. We would reduce him to a meek and mild savior, who demands nothing from us and gives everything to us; we would tame him, paint him as someone lovely to look at, pleasant to be with, wonderful to sing about.

O God, on Easter the thunder of your voice caused the stone to roll away from Christ's tomb. Now speak again, on behalf of Christ's people! Declare once again that this Christ, your servant and our Savior, has come to establish justice upon the earth.[83] *Justice*—not mere felicity, although he celebrates joy; not mere tolerance, although he celebrates diversity; not mere tranquillity, although he celebrates peace. No, he comes first to establish *justice,* and he shall not be stopped!

Tell it, Lord! Speak to us! Cause the rock of our self-concern to crumble, to tumble into the crevasse of our self-doubt! Make the ground shake beneath us, so that our feet shall dance, so that we shall leap up and run out the door, and carry mercy to a world awaiting its healing! Make the air tremble around us, so that our tongues shall shout, so that we shall sing from the rooftops, and announce good news to a world awaiting its release!

You can change us in a flash, Lord! In a word! Choose this moment! Give the command! And we will bear witness to you with our works of justice, filling the earth with deeds done in your name!

*Benediction.* I look, and I see a great multitude that no one can number, people from every nation and tribe and tongue, dancing on the mountaintop of God, clothed in brilliant robes of every color beneath the sun. And we the people become a rainbow, set upon the earth by the hand of God—the sign of God's covenant with every living creature, the visible promise of God's salvation, forever and forever, amen![84]

## Fifth Sunday of Easter

*Lections:* Acts 11:1-18; Psalm 148; Revelation 21:1-6; John 13:31-35

---

83 See Isaiah 42:1.
84 Inspired by Genesis 9:8-17.

*Call to Worship*

L: Let us who are lame spring up and dance!
P: Let us who are blind look up and dream!
L: Let us who are deaf hear and rejoice!
P: Let us who are mute shout and sing!
L: Our God will not be left without a faithful witness:
A: For we shall bless the name of the Lord forever and forever!

*Invocation.* O God, your dwelling is with your creation; your tabernacle is the earth, and your sanctuary, the sky. You uphold all who are falling, and you raise up all who are burdened; you are near to those who call upon you, and you are close to those who remain silent. We are grateful for your gracious presence, Lord, and we open ourselves to you. Claim us as your habitation, and make of us your holy city—a city where all your creatures may dwell without mourning, or crying, or pain, anymore.

*Litany*

L: Behold, our God is Alpha:
P: The Beginning, the Genesis, the End of the Old, the Start of the New: Let our God be praised!
L: Behold, our God is Birth:
P: The Womb, the Labor, the First Breath taken, the Cry of New Lungs: Let our God be glorified!
L: Behold, our God is Youth:
P: The Test, the Growing, the Desire for Freedom, the Need for Restraint: Let our God be praised!
L: Behold, our God is Age:
P: The Walk, the Changing, the Wisdom of the Past, the Hope for the Future: Let our God be glorified!
L: Behold, our God is Death:
P: The Letting Go, the Brilliant Light, the Departure from One World, the Destination of the Next: Let our God be praised!
L: Behold, our God is Omega:
P: The End, the Revelation, the Beginning of the New, the Finish of the Old: Let our God be glorified!

*Prayer for One Voice.* Almighty God, in Jesus you entered this life in the likeness of a human being and left it in the likeness of a divine being. In him you taught us the meaning of humanity and unveiled the mystery of divinity. In him you removed the sting of sin and shattered the fear of death. We come before you in the name of Christ our Lord, assured that, as we participate in his death to sin, we shall partake of his life in faith. Teach us, as you taught him, that just as we must live to die, we must die to live. And move us, as you moved the apostles, to interpret life on earth as an infiltration from heaven.

The apostles faced far greater dangers than we face, braved far more powerful enemies, took far more painful risks, and traveled far less friendly roads. Still they nourished the gospel to glorious flower. Can we make such a claim for ourselves, O God? Are our neighbors ever tempted to interpret our life among them as your descent into their midst? They look to us for your works, but sometimes they look in vain: Instead of faithful speech, they find faithless speech; instead of gracious deeds, selfish deeds; instead of support for the fallen, unconcern; instead of deliverance for the oppressed, indifference; instead of bread for the hungry, empty rhetoric; instead of evidence of the Crucified's resurrection, testimony to the resurrection of the crucifiers.

Our witness for Christ has not been as clear as it should have been or as compelling as it could have been. For this, O Lord, we are deeply ashamed and truly sorry. We pray that you will replace our shame with grace and our remorse with mercy; that henceforth, with singleness of purpose and purity of heart, we might bear faithful witness to the gospel and to you.

As we look at our world, we see multitudes of unhappy, discouraged, ill-clad, ill-fed, hungry, thirsty, and desperate people, many of whom are so fed up with the old earth that the best they can hope for is the old heaven. They despair of ever living on an earth where their hunger will be satisfied, their tears wiped away, their thirst quenched, and their longings fulfilled. Nevertheless, this is the new earth to whose creation Christ calls us. Grant us, O God, the compassion to envision such an earth, the will to work for it, and the grace to live on it.

Without price Christ has quenched our thirst with water from the fountain of life. He has shown us what your witnesses must be and what they must do. We pray, dear Lord, that your

97

spirit, the spirit that in Jesus produced the new being, will in us produce the new earth.

*Benediction.* Even as Christ, *without price,* has given us water from the fountain of life, let us, *without condition,* give to those in need. By this will the world know that we are Christ's disciples: if whoever turns to us does not perish, but is given abundant life.[85]

## Sixth Sunday of Easter

*Lections:* Acts 16:9-15; Psalm 67; Revelation 21:10, 22–22:5; John 14:23-29

*Call to Worship*

L:  If we love the Lord, we will honor God's will and serve our neighbor!

P:  Come, let us cherish the Lord our God, keeping our neighbor close to our heart!

L:  If we love God's will, we will honor our neighbor and serve the Lord!

P:  Come, let us cherish the will of God, keeping the Lord close to our heart!

L:  If we love our neighbor, we will honor the Lord and serve God's will!

P:  Come, let us cherish each child of God, keeping God's will close to our heart!

*Invocation.* O Counselor, come in Christ's name! Bring to our remembrance all that Jesus said and did, that we might be reminded of all that Christ charges us to say and do. We would fulfill that charge, we would keep that word, but our hearts are troubled; our minds, unsettled; our spirits, confused. Comfort us, quiet us, focus us, and then fill us with your saving power, that we might share the peace of Christ and spread the glory of God.

85  Inspired by John 3:16.

*Litany*

L: The Spirit carried me to a great, high mountain and showed me a vision of earth; I expected to see the holy city, descended to earth from heaven—

P: A city without need for sun or moon, having God's glory for eternal light.

L: But I saw instead a city shrouded by darkness, and peoples wandering in the gloom of night—[86]

P: Stumbling at noon as if it were twilight, refusing to know the ways of peace.[87]

L: I expected to see a holy place whose gates were open to everyone—

P: Whose doors could not close and whose lines could be crossed, since none were meant to be set apart.

L: But I saw instead a desolate place where violence reigned and corruption ruled—

P: Where gates were called Poverty instead of Praise, where borders were called Sin instead of Salvation.[88]

L: I expected to see a holy book whose pages held the names of the world's redeemed:

P: The afflicted, the broken, the poor, the captive, the sightless, the mournful.[89]

L: But I saw instead a book of curses, pronounced upon those who were hated and scorned—

P: Those whose names some ungodly hand would erase from the book of life.

L: "O Spirit," I cried, "take me down from this mountain; this terrible vision is too much for my eyes!"

P: But the Spirit said, "Why should you not see what I must see? Why hide from you the sight of sin when you do not spare me?"[90]

---

86  Inspired by Isaiah 60:2*a*.

87  See Isaiah 59:8, 10.

88  See Isaiah 60:18.

89  Inspired by Luke 4:17-18; Isaiah 61:1-2.

90  Inspired by Jeremiah 16:17.

L:   Therefore, I say: Cry, O earth! And wail, O world! For we, your people, have turned from God and left you alone and forsaken![91]

P:   O, hear the lament of a suffering creation: "Do I mean nothing, all you who pass by? Is there not one who will comfort me?"[92]

*Prayer for One Voice.* O Christ, the promise of whom nourished Israel's hope for the future, the life of whom inspired the apostles' mission to the world, the spirit of whom kindles our zeal for your reign, we come before you in gratitude. We thank you for your revelation—your revelation to us of God, and your revelation to us of ourselves. We thank you for making God more lovable and humanity more responsible; for making the law more flexible and duty more personal; for making religion less forbidding and goodness more appealing; for making revelation less a matter of the head and truth more a matter of the heart; for making God less an idea to be learned and more a presence to be experienced.

When we think of all the changes you have wrought, O Christ, we can only marvel at the difference you have made in history and humanity. Yet we are sobered by the even greater difference you *could* make, if only we would not stifle the spirit you let loose in the world—by putting uniformity of belief before unity of spirit; by putting correct doctrine before compassionate deed; by putting holy sacraments before human service; by putting yesterday's tradition before today's revelation; by putting the record of someone else's experience of God before our own experience of God. Forgive us, O Christ, for diminishing your influence. Grant us the grace to entrust our lives to the guidance of your Holy Spirit, that we might not only see your light, but follow.

Your prophets have told us of a great and wonderful city—a city to which darkness never comes, a city whose gates never close, a city in which all nations and peoples are welcome; a city whose Maker and Ruler is God, who governs its inhabi-

91   See Isaiah 14:31.
92   Inspired by Lamentations 1:4, 8, 12, 21.

tants with justice and judges them with equity. Deliver us from the temptation to dismiss this vision as if it had no relevance. Enable us to receive it as your message and as a pattern for the conduct of our life on earth. Put us in remembrance of your ways, O Christ, and incline our hearts to walk in them. Let us recall how you ministered to people not on the basis of your creed, but on the basis of their need; how you subordinated the demands of conventional piety to the claims of simple decency; how you put the alleviation of human misery ahead of the satisfaction of religious authority; how you spurned the applause of the mighty for service to the masses.

O Christ of God, you are not dead but alive and well. You live and reign over the new Jerusalem, the city in which there is no housing shortage, no unemployment, no lack of access to education or medical care, and food enough to go around. As you have opened its gates and your heart to us, send us forth to open its gates and our hearts to others.

*Benediction*
L: May the hand of the Spirit bless all peoples, and keep them;
P: May the face of the Spirit shine upon all peoples, and love them;
A: May the counsel of the Spirit guide all peoples, and bring them to lasting peace.[93]

## *Seventh Sunday of Easter*

*Lections:* Acts 16:16-34; Psalm 97; Revelation 22:12-14, 16-17, 20-21; John 17:20-26

*Call to Worship*
L: Let all who are thirsty come;
P: Let them drink of the water that has no price.
L: Let all who are hungry come;
P: Let them eat of the bread that has no cost.
L: All without money, come, buy, and eat![94]
P: Drink what is good, and delight in the Lord![95]

---

93 Inspired by Numbers 6:24-26.
94 See Isaiah 55:1.
95 Inspired by Isaiah 55:2.

*Invocation.* O Christ, you are the bright and morning star. You herald the dawn before we awaken. We fall asleep awaiting your ascent over the eastern horizon; yet all the night long, without our knowing, your light is rising within our hearts. It is time! Rouse us from our slumber, open the eyes of our souls, that, seeing you as never before, we might rejoice exceedingly with great joy.[96]

*Litany*

L: Blessed are they who seek living water—
P: The river that flows from the presence of God.
L: They shall find on its banks the tree of life,
P: Yielding its fruits of the Spirit:[97]
L: The fruits of faithfulness and love,
P: Of kindness and peace,
L: Of goodness and patience,
P: Of gentleness and mercy,
L: Of self-discipline and truth,
P: Of righteousness and joy.[98]
L: The Lord invites all to eat from this tree—[99]
P: No guardian angel will forbid it—[100]
L: For its leaves are for the healing of nations,[101]
P: And its fruits are for the mending of souls.
L: O blessed are they who seek living water—
A: And find by the river the tree of life, yielding its fruits of the Spirit!

*Prayer for One Voice.* Eternal God, whose rule spans the heavens and surrounds the earth, whose power bestows life and conquers death, whose love includes all generations and embraces all peoples, we come before you in the name of Christ our Lord.

You bless us with gifts we have yet to discover and powers we have yet to exercise; you set us in an environment where

---

96 Inspired by II Peter 1:19; Matthew 2:10.
97 See Ezekiel 47:12; Revelation 22:1, 2.
98 Inspired by Galatians 5:22-23; Ephesians 5:9; Philippians 1:11.
99 See Revelation 2:7.
100 Inspired by Genesis 3:24.
101 See Revelation 22:2.

they can flourish and among neighbors who can help decipher their mystery. We thank you, dear Lord, for the glory and grandeur of our existence and, above all, for Jesus Christ, in whom you confront us with the full development of these gifts and powers: the One who, by being born, brought heaven to earth and, by dying, raised earth to heaven; the One who, when he gave up life in his flesh-and-blood body, resumed life in his body of believers; the One who taught us that, if we would fulfill our human destiny, we must not forget our divine origin.

Yet how easily we forget his teaching! He taught that justice and righteousness are the foundations of your reign, yet our hearts continue to covet power and privilege. He taught that you are a jealous God, yet our idols continue to multiply. He taught that you are the God of all peoples, yet our prejudices continue to destroy us. He taught that you long to give the water of life to all who thirst, yet our greed continues to check its flow. Forgive us, O God, for trimming Christ's teaching to the size of our desires.

If it be that we cannot bear witness to Christ without cost to ourselves, we pray, O Lord, for the grace and strength to pay that cost without complaint or regret. Embolden us, as you did Paul and Silas, when they disturbed an entire city in defiance of Roman law. If, for the sake of your neglected children, you call upon us to disrupt the indifference of the powers that be, let us answer, like prophets, "Here are we, Lord; send us!"[102]

Let us not disturb the world merely for the sake of creating a disturbance, but to hasten the increase of justice and righteousness: by bringing food to the hungry, housing to the homeless, freedom to the oppressed, dignity to the abused, strength to the weak, and hope to the helpless. O God, where there is true peace, *your* peace—peace with justice—help us to keep it; but where there is false peace—peace with injustice—make us bold, for your sake and for the sake of its victims, to sound the prophet's cry for change.

---

102 See Isaiah 6:8.

*Benediction.* Let us go, remembering that we are one, even as the Lord our God is one. Let the faithfulness of our lives and the fullness of our love proclaim to the world that none of God's creatures is ever alone.

# Season After Pentecost

## Pentecost

*Lections:* Acts 2:1-21; Genesis 11:1-9 (alternate); Psalm 104:24-34; Romans 8:14-17; John 14:8-17, 25-27

*Call to Worship*

L: Children of God, sing to the Lord—

P: We shall sing to our Father while yet we have life!

L: Joint heirs with Christ, sing praise to your God—

P: We shall sing to our Mother while yet we have breath!

A: May the glory of God endure forever! May the world rejoice in the works of God's hands!

*Invocation.* O God, the earth is full of your creatures; in wisdom you have made us all, and you have delivered us into one another's care, asking only that we love one another as you first loved us.[103] But we have fostered discord rather than unity; contempt rather than respect; ignorance rather than love. Communities, peoples, creatures, lands, seas—they have been set apart, or torn apart, or driven apart, by conflicting claims and thoughtless ambitions.

You know our works and our thoughts, Lord. So do this day as you have promised: Gather together all our tribes and tongues, and restore us to harmony.[104] Reconcile us in your spirit of peace, and from new moon to new moon, and from sabbath to sabbath, all flesh shall worship your name.[105]

*Litany*

L: In the days before our pride, we said to one another:

P: "Come, let us make bricks!"

L: And we were content with our labor,

---

103 See I John 4:19.

104 Inspired by Isaiah 66:10.

105 See Isaiah 66:23.

P:    For bricks were needed for the building of houses and the laying of roads.

L:    But when our houses were built and our roads were laid, our hearts swelled with pride. Then we proposed to one another:

P:    "Come, let us raise a tower whose top will touch the sky!"

L:    In those days we began to grow restless in our labor,

P:    For the tower was never high enough, and the base was never broad enough;

L:    The workday was never long enough, and the effort was never great enough. Then our hearts swelled to bursting, and we schemed with one another:

P:    "Come, let us make a name for ourselves!"

L:    And in those days we grew ruthless in our labor,

P:    For the bricks were never ample enough, and the mortar was never thick enough;

L:    The overseers were never demanding enough, and the workers were never ambitious enough. Then our hearts were hardened, and we screamed at one another:

P:    "Double the number of bricks to be made—the workers are lazy, their hands are idle!"

L:    Then the people murmured and groaned in their bondage, and they cried to God for help—[106]

P:    And, hearing their cries, God scattered our pride across the face of the earth.

A:    O Lord, have compassion and gather us in. Prosper the works of those who love you, until our sinful hearts come home with all their soul and strength.[107]

*Prayer for One Voice.* O God, who is present with us in more ways than we can count—turning confusion into order, condemnation into deliverance, and isolation into fellowship—we thank you for all the ways you are present. We especially thank you for taking the initiative in bringing us together: in creation, by stamping your image upon us; in Christ, by manifesting your love for us; and at Pentecost, by sending your spirit upon

---

[106] Inspired by Exodus 4:21; 5:7-9; 2:23-24.
[107] Entire litany inspired by Genesis 11:1-9.

us. You have spared no effort in your search for us, and for this, O God, we give thanks.

Yet we must plead guilty to not returning the compliment. Not only do we fail to seek you as you seek us, but we run from you after you find us. Instead of turning to you for counsel, we turn to others; instead of looking to Christ for an example, we imitate our neighbors; instead of seeking a common tongue, we multiply the tongues of pride. As a consequence, we are confused persons in the midst of a confused people, speaking not the one tongue of a common love but the many tongues of private ambition, working not to bring humanity together but to keep it apart.

Forgive us, O God, for thus betraying your purpose: for failing to see that we cannot go it alone without going astray; that we can realize your destiny for us only in community; and that the Holy Spirit, which is working to effect our union with you in heaven, is also working to effect our union with our neighbors on earth.

O God, let your spirit descend upon us as it descended upon the crowds in Jerusalem. Let it strike us as a mighty wind, blowing away the chaff of pride. Let it burn within us as a tongue of fire, consuming the dross of selfishness. And let it lead us forth into the world, proclaiming the dawn in which the young see visions and the old dream dreams, and pursuing your mission in a community bent on becoming the body of Christ.

We are your children, O Lord, and joint heirs with Christ to all your gracious gifts. Let us not betray our heritage. As Christ served his heritage by revealing you to others, let us serve ours by revealing him to others. And as his neighbors came to know you through him, let ours come to know him through us.

O God, let us never forget that the church of Jesus Christ is as dependent upon the Spirit for its life as for its birth. It is the Spirit who gives us the faith to envision one world, the motivation to love its peoples, the determination to discern their needs, and the will to serve them in the name of Christ our Savior. So we pray not merely for an increase in the membership of the church, but for the outpouring of your spirit upon its members. Let it come upon us with the power that compels, the truth that convicts, and the love that converts. Let Pentecost cease to be a past to be remembered and become again a present to be experienced.

*Benediction.* Yesterday we slaved in the shadow of Babel. Today we are freed by Pentecost's fire. Let our pride divide us no longer; let the Spirit unite us forever. The peace of God I leave with you; the peace of God I give unto you. Let not your hearts be troubled, neither let them be afraid.

### First Sunday After Pentecost
*Trinity Sunday*

*Lections:* Proverbs 8:22-31; Psalm 8; Romans 5:1-5; John 16:12-15

*Call to Worship*

L: I am Wisdom; my mouth utters truth. Do you not hear my call?

P: Your voice is raised in the way of righteousness; in the path of justice you have taken your stand.

L: To you I cry, and my cry is to all: O simple ones, learn prudence; O foolish ones, take heed!

P: We will take your instruction instead of silver, and knowledge of you rather than gold; for you, O Wisdom, are better than jewels, and nothing we covet compares with your glory![108]

*Invocation.* O Wisdom, you have built your house and set your table; you have invited us into your presence, saying, "Come, eat of my bread and drink of my wine. Know me, and live, and walk in the way of insight."

So we gather in your dwelling place, Spirit: Guide us, we pray, into truth. Instruct us in righteousness, and justice, and equity, helping us to understand your proverbs and to unravel your riddles. We seek you diligently; let us find you, as you have promised.[109]

---

108 See Proverbs 8:1-11, 20.
109 See Proverbs 9:1-6; 1:3, 6; 8:17.

*Litany*

L:  O Lord, our God, how majestic is your name in all the earth!

M:  You whose glory above the heavens is chanted by the mouth of babes and infants—

W:  You whose fingers established the heavens, the sun, the moon, and the stars—

M:  Who are humans that you are mindful of them?

W:  And who are mortals that you care for them?

M:  Why have you crowned us with glory and honor?

W:  Why have you made us little less than yourself?

M:  Why have you given us Wisdom for a teacher?

W:  She was brought forth before the world began—

M:  When deserts had no sand and rivers had no water;

W:  When mountains had no shape and prairies had no form;

M:  When land had no foundation and oceans had no shore;

W:  When earth had no horizon and heaven had no hue.

M:  She has always worked beside you, a gifted artisan,

W:  Rejoicing with you in creation, and making all things new.[110]

M:  O let us not forsake her, our Keeper and our Guide—

W:  For her ways are ways of justice, and all her paths are peace![111]

A:  O Lord, our God, how majestic is the name of Wisdom in all the earth!

*Prayer for One Voice.* Almighty and eternal God, whose mystery defies our knowledge yet defines our meaning, whose love transcends our understanding yet transforms our existence, and whose power incites our fear yet inspires our faith, we praise your holy name. We pray that you will grant us a fuller vision of yourself and the strength so to live that we shall reveal you as clearly as we see you.

No matter in what direction we look, whether up or down or around or within, the evidence of your handiwork confronts us. No matter what we behold—whether the spacious heavens above us, the good earth beneath us, the teeming creatures around us, or the aspiring person within us—your wisdom

---

110 Inspired by Revelation 21:5.
111 Inspired by Proverbs 4:6; 3:17.

overwhelms us. We cannot contemplate anything you have made without standing in awe of its Maker. You are indeed a great and wise God, O Lord, but we adore you for something greater than your greatness and wiser than your wisdom. Above all, we adore you for the love that will not let us go, the love that has pursued us from the the time we began to turn a wilderness into civilization until we started turning civilization back into wilderness. It is the love that tells us that, no matter how badly we deface your image, we can never destroy it. It is the love that assures us that, just as the spirit of Christ moved in the church of yesterday, it moves in the church of today.

Yet we must confess, O Lord, that our conduct as often impresses our neighbors with the absence of Christ as with his presence. While applauding his call for peacemaking, we exercise our preference for troublemaking. While praising his outcries against oppressors, we withhold our support for the oppressed. While admiring his union of belief and behavior, we overlook our tendency to separate them. While hailing his demand for compassion, we press our demand for retribution. While commending his practice of thinking with his heart, we indulge our habit of thinking with our spleen.

O God, forgive us for all the ways we contribute to the world's sense of Christ's absence. Pour out your spirit upon us, that his presence might again be felt moving among us, making us whole and making us one. Take from us our estrangement from the poor, the first to whom Christ brought the good news. Take from us our insensitivity to the brokenhearted, the first to whom Christ brought healing. Take from us our unconcern for the captive, the first to whom Christ brought liberty. Take from us our disdain for the sorrowful, the first to whom Christ brought comfort.

O Lord, come among us now as before. Come among us, as in creation, to stamp your image on all your creatures. Come among us, as in Christ, to offer your love to your creatures gone wrong. Come among us, as at Pentecost, to breathe your blessing upon your creatures united in fellowship, that we might be encouraged by one another's faith.[112]

---

112 See Romans 1:12.

*Benediction.* Let all who suffer hear and rejoice! They will not suffer alone. We shall be with them, bearing all things, believing all things, enduring all things, and hoping all things.[113] This great hope shall not disappoint, for love has been poured into our hearts through the spirit of the Lord.

### *Sunday Between May 29 and June 4 Inclusive*
### *(if after Trinity Sunday)*

*Lections:* I Kings 18:20-21 (22-29), 30-39; Psalm 96; Galatians 1:1-12; Luke 7:1-10

*Call to Worship*
L:  Spread your open hands toward heaven—
P:  Sing to the Lord a new song!
L:  The Lord is like no other God—
P:  Sing to the Lord, all the earth!
L:  Come together to pray and praise:
P:  The Lord has made us—*Hallelujah!* To the Lord we belong, forever—*Amen!*

*Invocation.* O Lord, hear us in your habitation; listen to us in your dwelling place! Whatever our age, or race, or homeland, or class, or gender, or intelligence, or ability, or creed, you have promised to show us love: to heal us when we are wounded, to protect us when we are vulnerable, to come to us when we are alone. We stand now in need of your steadfast love; do not disappoint us!

*Litany*
L:  O Spirit, help us so to serve you, that all the world might hear and rejoice in the greatness of your name:
W:  Lord of hosts, God of gods, Ruler of glory, Judge of earth, Lover of justice, Avenger of wrong;
M:  Upholder of life, Lifter of heads, Parent to the orphan, Protector of the weak;
A:  Maker, Savior, Redeemer, Deliverer, Helper, Shepherd, Keeper, Midwife, sheltering Wings, forgiving God!

---

113 Inspired by I Corinthians 13:7.

L:  O Spirit, help us so to serve you, that all the world might hear and rejoice in the greatness of your love:

W:  The love that opens, stretches forth, anoints, lifts up, rescues, saves;

M:  The love that leads, abides, receives our spirits, helps, holds our times;

A:  The love that holds the cup of agony—a strong love, exalted, high, but forgotten!

L:  O Spirit, help us so to serve you, that all the world might hear and rejoice in the greatness of your love:

W:  The love that creates the heavens and earth and all who dwell therein, that performs great signs and wonders;

M:  The love that rules, that triumphs, that scatters the wicked and makes them still;

A:  The love that brings slaves out of bondage, that gathers the lambs and all who are scattered—the love that is bared before all the nations![114]

*Prayer for One Voice.* Eternal God, who in Jesus Christ redeems us from the sin that drives us apart and reconciles us with the love that brings us together, we thank you for him who has made us your partners in covenant. We bless you for the vision with which you bless us through him: for the vision of yourself, whose love for all does not diminish your love for each; for the vision of us as individuals, whose move away from you does not slow your move toward us; for the vision of the community of believers, whose history of division does not alter your desire for union; and for the vision of the world, whose clamor for power does not silence your demand for justice.

O God, grant us the faith of Solomon's prayer: the faith that calls the temple not by the builder's name but by your name; the faith that looks not within the temple but beyond for your dwelling place; the faith that longs for the temple to become a house of prayer—not for one people but for all the peoples of the earth.

Unfortunately, our faith in Christ has often been no match for Solomon's prayer. We sing of Christ for all the world, but the world we have in mind is much smaller than the world for

---

114 The imagery in this prayer was gleaned primarily from the Psalms.

112

which Solomon prayed. It is not the world of "all the peoples of the earth," but only some of them—those of them who think as we think, feel as we feel, worship as we worship, and live as we live.

Forgive us, O God, not only for shrinking your world to the size of our prejudices, but for reducing Christ to the level of our preferences. Too often we turn your Christ into a Christ of our own creation: a Christ too narrow to tolerate any behavior we do not approve; to sanction any belief we do not hold; to welcome any person we do not like; to permit any worship we do not practice.

O God, you have made us in your image. Forgive us for remaking the world in ours. You have made Christ the church's one foundation. Forgive us for trying to build it on another. Transform us, O Lord. Grant us the grace so to represent the Christ you have sent that the world might receive your glorious gospel, obey your great commandments, and worship your holy name.

*Benediction.* As we leave this place, let us be committed to living the gospel, seeking not human favor but divine approval. And let us remember that it is not submission before God, but *devotion to* God, to which we are called in the name of Christ.

## *Sunday Between June 5 and June 11 Inclusive*
### *(if after Trinity Sunday)*

*Lections:* I Kings 17:8-16 (17-24); Psalm 146; Galatians 1:11-24; Luke 7:11-17

*Call to Worship*

L: O servants of God, sing praise to the Lord,

P: Who raises the poor from the dust and lifts the needy from the pit!

A: Who is like the Lord of heaven? Blessed be the name of the Lord, from the rising of the sun to its setting!

L: O servants of God, sing praise to the Lord,

P: Who causes the lowly to sit with the proud and makes the haughty to be humbled!

A: Who is like the Lord of earth? Blessed be the name of the Lord, from this time forth and for evermore!

113

*Invocation.* Visit us, O Christ! Strengthen us in our inmost being, that, grounded in your spirit, we might comprehend the breadth and length and height and depth of your love. Dwell in our hearts, that, filled with the fullness of God, we might understand the faith that surpasses knowledge.[115] Empower us, O Savior, that all the world might glorify your name because of your gracious works!

*Litany*

L:  O Lord, hear my groaning! Hear the lament of your suffering Earth![116] For I will no longer restrain my mouth; I will complain in the anguish of my spirit and speak from the distress of my soul.

W:  My winds cry, "Violence!" but no one makes peace; my tempests scream "Sin!" but no one seeks justice.

M:  My life is delivered into the hands of the wicked; my wounds and my grief multiply without cause.

W:  They shrivel me up and tear me down; they gnash their teeth and strike me;

M:  They slash my body—the ground is red with my blood, though my hands are innocent and my prayer is pure.

W:  Ask the beasts, Lord, and they will tell you; ask the birds of the air, or the plants of the ground—

M:  Even the fish of the sea understand what human hands have done; even they know who holds my fate.

W:  O how can my life be saved from destruction?

M:  If they cause me to die, shall I live again?

W:  Who are humans to torment me so? Where were they when you laid my foundations? Did they make the clouds my swaddling clothes? Did they teach the stars to sing lullabies?

M:  Have they ever laid eyes upon the home of my winds? Have they ever dispatched the rains to my deserts, or frozen the waters of my deep? Have they ever caused the robin to fly to the south, or provided the raven with food for her young?

---

115 Inspired by Ephesians 3:15-19.
116 Inspired by Romans 8:22.

W: O that these days were like days of old, when *you* guarded my life and watched over me;

M: If only you would wrap me in righteousness once more, and cover me again with the robe of justice![117]

L: O Lord, hear my groaning! Hear the lament of your sorrowful Earth!

A: O Lord, I am dying! Hear my prayer, and return to me the breath of life!

*Prayer for One Voice.* O God of glory and God of grace, whose majesty adorns the heavens and whose mercy fills the earth, who needs nothing we can give yet gives us everything we need, who silences the shouts of the proud yet amplifies the whispers of the humble, we come before you in awe and gratitude. We stand in awe of the glory with which you bless the universe; we bow in gratitude for the light with which you illumine our life.

When we ponder the awful power of nature—the winds of the tornado, the waves of the hurricane, the rumblings of the earthquake—we are reminded not only of your incredible might but of our incredible weakness. In the face of such power, we are helpless. But once nature's fury has subsided and her face is again creased with a smile, we are struck not only by your incredible gentleness but by our incredible strength.

O Lord, we do not know whether the day will come when we can fully harness the power of nature. Yet we can surely understand it better, so that we are able to reduce its capacity for destruction. Quicken our thirst for such understanding, but deliver us from the temptation to dwell only upon nature's power for destruction. Let us celebrate her power for blessing and her potential for healing.

We thank you, O Lord, for the healing power of nature. Help us to bring those in need of healing within her reach. You have given us not only enough fertile land to produce goods adequate for the human family, but the science of agriculture for increasing the supply. Help us to use this science for the sake

---

117 Inspired by Job 7:11; 19:7; 9:17-24; 16:8-17; 12:7-10; 9:2; 14:14; 38; 39; 29:2; 21:14-16.

115

of your children. You have given us not only enough food to eliminate hunger, but the science of nutrition for maximizing its benefits. Help us to use this science for the sake of your children. You have given us not only antidotes to attack disease, but the science of medicine for spreading health. Help us to use this science for the sake of your children.

O God, we are grateful for the healing power you mediate through nature. We are even more grateful for the healing presence you mediate through people: through those who speak a comforting word in times of mourning; those who lend a helping hand in times of suffering; those who play a supporting role in times of loneliness; those who offer a saving loan in times of need; those who suggest a clarifying course in times of confusion. Join our resources to yours, and make us mediators of your healing presence, that the world might praise you all the day, every day.

*Benediction.* In this place, the Lord has confronted us with the gospel; now let us proclaim the good news to the world. Let us so live that the lives of the most lowly might be touched and healed by the Spirit of the Most High.

## Sunday Between June 12 and June 18 Inclusive
### (if after Trinity Sunday)

*Lections:* I Kings 21:1-10 (11-14), 15-21*a*; Psalm 5:1-8; Galatians 2:15-21; Luke 7:36–8:3

*Call to Worship*
L: O people, enter the house of God—
P: Let the Spirit wash your feet with tears, and wipe them with her hair.
L: From the moment you come into her presence,
P: She will never cease to kiss your feet, and anoint them with fine ointment.
A: Do we not know what Spirit this is who dares to touch us so? Our sin is great, but her love is greater; and greater, too, shall be *our* love, when forgiveness is received!

*Invocation.* As weary travelers long for soothing waters, so our soul longs for you, O God. Our soul *thirsts* for you, the living water; we pray, give us a drink, and we will never thirst again! Come, let us partake of you, and a spring of water will rush up within us, welling up to eternal life.[118]

*Litany*

L: Arise and eat, O people of God!

P: Let us partake of the food of the Spirit, for God has set us on a journey: The highway is infinity; its destination, eternity!

L: Arise and eat, or the journey will be too long for you!

P: Let us partake of the food of the Spirit, for God has called us to a mission: The task is faithfulness; its fulfillment, God's reign!

L: Arise and eat, or the mission will be too hard for you!

P: Let us partake of the food of the Spirit, for God has given us a message: The word is life; its story, salvation!

L: Arise and eat, or the message will be too wonderful for you!

P: Let us partake of the food of the Spirit, for God has granted us knowledge: The wisdom is compassion; its teaching, mercy!

L: Arise and eat, or the knowledge will be too wondrous for you!

P: A journey, a mission, a message, and knowledge: Let us give thanks for the bread and break it, and partake of the loaf together!

L: Arise and eat, O people of God!

A: Let us partake, all of us together; for this is the bread of our covenant with God, broken for us all!

*Prayer for One Voice.* Gracious God, into whose presence we come with confidence because you come to us in grace, we pause now, as pilgrims on a journey, for renewal and direction. Others have offered us water for our thirst, but it is not quenched; food for our hunger, but it is not satisfied; a map for our guidance, but it is not clear. So now we come unto you, for you have the water that can quench our thirst, and we know that you will give us to drink; you have the food that can satisfy

---

118 Inspired by John 4:7-15.

our hunger, and we know that you will give us to eat; you have the map that can help us find the way home, and we know that you will give us to see.

We thank you, dear Lord, not only for the gifts with which you bless us, but for the welcome with which you greet us. Just as your gifts tell us that you are glad to be our host, your welcome tells us that you are ready to be our guide; and this is what we pilgrims of the way desire above all else.

Yet we turn from you more often than we return to you. Although our meetings with you never fail to renew us, they take place all too rarely. We allow them to become spasmodic and occasional. We long for you, not as those who exalt in your name, but as the addict for a quick fix; not as the pioneer for a new homeland, but as the traveler for overnight accommodation; not as the truth-seeker for wisdom, but as the novelty-hunter for entertainment. When you ask, "Why have you forgotten me, O my people?" we answer, "Why, O Lord, have you forgotten *us?* Why do many of us, who love and worship you, fare less well than many who do not? Does our piety count for nothing? Are our prayers and presence in this place of no consequence?"

Teach us, dear Lord, that you call us not for our glorification but for yours. Teach us that you sanctify us not for our sake but for the sake of our neighbors. Awaken us to our brothers and sisters, for whose fulfillment you anoint us as your servants. Let us not envy them if you love them before they deserve it, lest we forget that you love us before *we* deserve it.

We thank you, O God, for reminding us how much we are like others. And we thank you, even more, for reminding us how important others are to you: how you love them as deeply as you love us; how you long for them to become one—not only with us but with you. Let us tarry no longer. Enlist us now, dear Lord, as co-laborers with you in breaking down the dividing walls of hostility, whether between them and us or between ourselves and you.

*Benediction.* Now, therefore, let us commit our lives to God, that the world might see our acts of mercy and know that it is not *we* who live and work, but the forgiving and reconciling Christ who lives and works in us.

## Sunday Between June 19 and June 25 Inclusive
### (if after Trinity Sunday)

*Lections:* I Kings 19:1-4 (5-7), 8-15a; Psalm 42 and 43; Galatians 3:23-29; Luke 8:26-39

*Call to Worship*

. L: Daughters and sons of God, why are you here?

P: We have gathered on the seventh day to march around the walls of hate: Hear the tramping of our feet! Hear the blaring of our trumpets! Hear the ringing of our hammers! Hear the shouting of our voices! O walls, tumble down!

A: This world is *one!* No wall can divide us; no wall shall stand! With Christ as our peace, and God as our power, all walls shall crumble before us![119]

*Invocation.* O Christ, the light that illumines the night and the truth that frees the bound, lead us in true worship: in defending the rights of the powerless and setting free the oppressed; in sharing bread with the hungry and offering shelter to the homeless; in giving clothing to the naked and bringing healing to the wounded. Reveal the glory of true faithfulness; let your justice break forth like the dawn. *You* shall be our everlasting light, and we will be your witnesses, and all the days of mourning shall end.[120]     .

*Litany*

L: Come, let us stand upon the mountain and wait for God to join us.

P: Let us stand firm, though the wind blow strong against us and hurl at us without pity. Though the wind clap its hands and hiss at us, though it shake the trees and swirl the dust, we will not be made to flee.[121]

L: For behold, our God is not in the wind: This is a wind that *we* have sown, and the whirlwind we reap.[122]

---

119 Inspired by Joshua 6; see also Ephesians 2:14.
120 See Isaiah 58:6-8; 60:19-20.
121 Inspired by Job 27:21.
122 See Hosea 8:7.

P: Let us stand firm, though an earthquake split the rocks beneath us and even the heavens tremble.[123] Though the earth be utterly broken apart, though it sway and wobble upon its foundations, we will not be made to flee.[124]

L: For behold, our God is not in the earthquake: This is an earthquake *we* have triggered, and the havoc we suffer.

P: Let us stand firm, though a fire ignite the air around us and even the rivers burn. Though the flames singe our hair and choke our breath, though they crackle and spit and laugh in our face, we will not be made to flee.

L: For behold, our God is not in the fire: This is a fire that *we* have kindled,[125] and the conflagration we feed.

P: And after the fire we shall tremble, hearing a still small voice; and the voice shall cause all wars to cease—one sentence shall break the bow, one word shall shatter the spear—

A: And behold, the voice shall be with us, saying: "Be still, and know that I am God!"[126]

*Prayer for One Voice.* O God of awesome power and disquieting silence, we bow in adoration before you, grateful for the loud thunder that removes you far from us and for the gentle whisper that draws you close to us. Through the ages you have come to us in tones that muffled the sound of your presence, in visions that dimmed the sight of your appearance, and in forms that defied the touch of your being. Yet we continue to look for you, as did Elijah, in the rushing wind, the trembling earth, and the streaking fire, but we are disappointed until we stop looking and learn to listen: until we stop looking for your cosmic fireworks and learn to listen for a gentle whisper.

Help us, O God, to learn how to listen, especially to you. Forgive us for insisting not only on the last word but the first word; for reporting to you how our neighbors victimize us, as if you were unaware of their transgression; for dictating to you how you can help us, as if you were unaware of our need; for reminding you how often justice is frustrated, as if you were

---

123 Inspired by Isaiah 13:13.
124 See Isaiah 24:18-20.
125 Inspired by Isaiah 50:11.
126 Inspired by Psalm 46:9-10.

unaware of its miscarriage; for advising you how swift retribution must be, as if our times were not in your hands.

O Lord, forgive our shameless presumption. Not only do we seek to put words in your mouth, but we try to wrench the reins of authority from your hand. We are unwilling to wait for your judgment, preferring to assert our own; unwilling to trust your justice, preferring to administer our own; unwilling to respect your schedule, preferring to set our own. Forgive our impatience, and grant us the humility to stop thinking of ourselves more highly than we should and to start thinking of you as highly as we ought.

O Lord, teach us the beauty of silence, especially in your presence, until we learn the ways of the divine/human dialogue. Break the silence with a word of grace until we join the conversation with an act of faith; until we are ready to grant you the last word; until we recognize that you, and you alone, may set the time for speaking that word.

This we pray, dear God, for the sake of all your children. We will not do right by them until we see them as you see them and esteem them as you esteem them. Deliver us from the temptation to give them what they deserve, rather than what they need. Enable us to go to others in their need as you come to us in ours. As you give yourself for us, let us give ourselves for our neighbors.

*Benediction*

L:  Sons and daughters of God, why are you here?

P:  Let us go forth into the world; let us break down every wall of hate! Tramp, O feet! Blare, O trumpets! Ring, O hammers! Shout, O voices!

A:  This world is *one!* No wall shall stand! With Christ as our peace, and God as our power, all walls shall fall by the work of our hands![127]

### *Sunday Between June 26 and July 2 Inclusive*

*Lections:* II Kings 2:1-2, 6-14; Psalm 77:1-2, 11-20; Galatians 5:1, 13-25; Luke 9:51-62

---

127 Inspired by Joshua 6; see also Ephesians 2:14.

# LITANIES AND OTHER PRAYERS

*Call to Worship*

L: For freedom Christ has set us free;

P: Deliver us, Lord, from the demands of our world!

L: To service God has called us all;

P: Yoke us, Lord, to the needs of your world—and this for the sake of your gospel![128]

*Invocation.* O God, we have rejoiced in the stories of your faithfulness. We pray that you will so increase the hearing of our ears, the perception of our eyes, the compassion of our hearts, and the willingness of our hands, that stories of *our* faithfulness might reach your ears, and you, too, might rejoice.

*Litany*

L: O people, walk in my spirit, and bear the fruit of self-control—

P: We would follow you, Lord, but first: These people who offend us, shall we not bid fire to rain down from heaven upon them?

L: Walk in my spirit, and bear the fruit of gentleness—

P: We would follow you, Lord, but first: This blind man who begs us, shall we not command him to be silent?

L: Walk in my spirit, and bear the fruit of faithfulness—

P: We would follow you, Lord, but first: This hungry crowd that hounds us, shall we not send them home?[129]

L: Walk in my spirit, and bear the fruit of goodness—

P: We would follow you, Lord, but first: These disciples who are with us, shall we not have more power than they?[130]

L: Walk in my spirit, and bear the fruit of patience—

P: We would follow you, Lord, but first: These children who approach us, shall we not chase them away?

L: Walk in my spirit, and bear the fruit of peace—

P: We would follow you, Lord, but first: These foes who confront us, shall we not draw our swords?

L: Walk in my spirit, and bear the fruit of love—

[128] See I Corinthians 9:19 and 9:23.

[129] See Luke 18:35-39; Matthew 14:15.

[130] Inspired by Luke 22:24-27.

P:  We would follow you, Lord, but first: This lowly woman
who pleads for her daughter, shall we not rebuke her?[131]
L:  O faithless and perverse generation, how long am I to
bear with you? If you will not follow and serve, send
the woman to me![132]

*Prayer for One Voice.* O God of gracious word and mighty deed,
we thank you for your holy presence. It has been the staff of
our life and the source of our faith from the day of our birth,
and from generation to generation of all those who have gone
before us. When the Israelites threatened to trade you for alien
gods, you sent prophets to herald the perils of idolatry. When
the powerful began to exploit the weak, you raised up lawgivers to proclaim the demands of justice. Beg as we may to be
free of the watchful eye of heaven, you will not leave us alone.
We thank you, dear Lord, for your refusal to respect our
privacy. We thank you, too, that we are never so fully present
to ourselves as when you are fully present to us.

Yet we must confess, O God, that we, like our ancestors,
confuse your presence with that of an alien deity. We fill your
mouth with words that are less than gracious. We ascribe to
you deeds that are less than noble. We turn our enemies into
your enemies, putting our sword into your hand. We pillage
their land for our own use, crediting you with the transfer of
title. We justify your preferential treatment of us, claiming
your hatred for them. Shamelessly, we identify our passions
with yours, shrinking your compassion to the size of ours.

O God, forgive our indulgence of the works of the flesh that
Christ crucified, and for our crucifixion of the works of the spirit
that Christ indulged. Let us not forget that the freedom for which
Christ set us free is not the freedom through power to become
masters but the freedom through love to become servants.

Help us, O God, to become faithful servants—servants who
will inspire others to heed your summons without hesitation;
servants who will make a difference in the world as in the
church. Let us, as when we first believed, put our hand to the

131 See Matthew 19:13; Mark 14:47; Matthew 15:22-23.
132 Inspired by Matthew 17:17.

plow and, without looking back, use our freedom to multiply the fruits of your spirit.

*Benediction.* O people, set your face steadfastly toward the world. Greet the call of Christ not with an excuse but with enthusiasm, that your faithfulness might testify to the faithfulness of God.

## Sunday Between July 3 and July 9 Inclusive

*Lections:* II Kings 5:1-14; Psalm 30; Galatians 6:1-16; Luke 10:1-11, 16-20

*Call to Worship*
L: O neighbors, have you not heard the news? The realm of God is drawing near!
P: Mustard seeds are falling around us, scattered by the Spirit's hand!
L: Come, let us tend and water them, and see that none is choked by thorns;
P: Come, let us sing, and the seeds will grow tall, and even the birds shall build nests in the branches![133]

*Invocation.* Give ear to our words, O God; hearken to our cries! To *you* we pray—though you are a God who takes no delight in boasting, and we have been less than humble; though you are a God who takes no delight in deceit, and we have been less than honest; though you are a God who takes no delight in violence, and we have been less than just.

Humble our pride, Lord, and we will boast only of you.[134] Straighten our tongues, and we will shout your truth from the rooftops. Rule our spirits, and we will serve you, and study war no more.[135]

*Litany*
L: O God, make of us a new creation,
P: And your world will sing you a love song!

133 See Matthew 13:7; Luke 13:18-19.
134 See II Corinthians 10:17.
135 Inspired by Matthew 10:27; Isaiah 2:4.

L: We are your land, Lord: Clear us of stones!
P: Cultivate us, and plant us with choice vines!
L: Wait for us to yield good fruit:
P: Rise up early, and prune our branches;
L: Send our roots deep beside living waters,
P: And command the clouds to rain!
L: We will not fear the heat of summer,
P: Nor become anxious in the year of drought;
L: Our leaves will stay green, our fruit will hang heavy—
P: We will not cease to produce your bounty.
L: In you we have placed our trust, O Lord;
P: We will not bear grapes that are wild and bitter!
L: O God, make of us a new creation,
P: Make us the work of your hands—
L: And when you look for justice, you will not see bloodshed;
P: When you listen for righteousness, you will not hear a cry!
A: You, our Maker, will be glorified,[136] and the world you have made will be saved![137]

*Prayer for One Voice.* Gracious God, who withholds from us nothing that we might serve you in everything, we thank you for welcoming us to membership in your family and to partnership in your mission. We thank you, too, that even while denying us equality with your person, you encourage our pursuit of your purpose. And we thank you that you never weary of giving us clues as to what that purpose is and how we might advance it.

O God, through your lawgivers and prophets you demonstrated your displeasure with wickedness, boastfulness, deceitfulness, and bloodthirstiness. And when we turned your hatred of evil into a hatred of evildoers, you spoke a corrective word through Jesus, making clear that you seek the destruction not of the sinful but of sin, not of the deceitful but of deceit, not of the violent but of violence.

But we have been slow to understand. We continue to divide the world into hostile camps, one pious and the other profane,

136 See Isaiah 60:21; 61:3.
137 Litany inspired by Isaiah 5:1-7; Jeremiah 17:7-8.

125

one law-observing and the other law-breaking, one faithful and the other faithless, one humble and the other proud. Ignoring Christ's reminder that he came to call not the well but the sinful to repentance, we identify ourselves as the well and others as the sinful, dehumanizing them and echoing the psalmist's cry for their punishment. We dismiss them as if you could not redeem them; we treat them as if you did not create them.

O Lord, how we wish that we had had nothing to do with the sowing of what we are reaping! But we were there when the seeds of smug superiority were scattered among the underprivileged, the underfed, and the undervalued. Try as we may, we cannot wash our hands of all blame for the harvest of shame they have produced. We can only pray for the strength to survive this harvest and, once it is past, for the wisdom to sow seed that will yield a very different harvest.

The fields are indeed white unto harvest, O God. The seeds of our bigotry and intolerance and selfishness and indifference have yielded bountiful crops. The laborers in the fields grow faint. We pray, therefore, to the Lord of the harvest: Raise up more laborers to destroy the fruit of this planting, that we might prepare the soil for the next.

*Benediction.* Go your way, and may the peace of Christ and the mercy of God go with you. Do not lose heart, do not grow weary; do good to all without ceasing, and the Spirit will harvest the fruit of your labors.

## Sunday Between July 10 and July 16 Inclusive

*Lections:* Amos 7:7-17; Psalm 82; Colossians 1:1-14; Luke 10:25-37

*Call to Worship*
L:  Brothers and sisters, have you loved your neighbor? Have you stopped by the road and bandaged the wounded, or have you passed by on the other side?
P:  The Lord is acquainted with all our ways!
L:  Sisters and brothers, have you loved your God? Have you carried the afflicted to a place of rest, or have you turned your back and hurried on?
P:  The Lord is acquainted with all our ways!

L: Come to God, that you might learn to show mercy. Come to God, that you might *receive* mercy.

P: Let the Lord teach us how our hearts can love—with all their soul and strength and mind!

*Invocation.* O Christ, who broke down the wall between worship in the sanctuary and duty in the marketplace, we come before you today with a guilty conscience. We wish we could plead innocent of the charge of seeking to raise this wall anew. But we know, even as you know, O Lord, of our bent to judge unjustly, denying justice to the weak and showing partiality to the wicked. Wherefore, we ask, O Lord, for your forgiveness and, after that, for the transformation alike of our understanding and our will. Search us and try us, O God, that we might not only face but flee the spirit of the priest and Levite that dwells within us; and that, confronted by the challenge of the Samaritan, we might heed your words to go and do likewise.

## Litany

L: O children in the womb and prophets yet unborn, ask how we might enable the gospel to bear fruit throughout the whole earth.

W: Let there be day, and let there be night; let them dwell together in peace.

M: Let there be clouds in the blue of the heavens; let them blanket the earth with care.

W: Let there be lands, and let there be waters; let them have abundant life, like that they amply give.

M: Let there be sun and moon and stars; let them watch over the peoples of earth and lead them all to freedom.

W: Let there be fish in the sea and birds in the sky, beasts in the forest and cattle in the field;

M: Let them be fruitful and multiply, like plants and trees that yield their seed, according to their kind.

W: Let there be men, and let there be women; and let them live in the image of God, allowing the world to thrive.

L: O children in the womb and prophets yet unborn, we shall do what you ask as long as we have breath. 'Til this generation yields place to the next, our hands are holding the fate of your birth; our hands are holding the fate of the earth!

A:   May the Lord our God behold what is done; may the Lord our God declare the work good![138]

*Prayer for One Voice.* O Christ, whose wisdom we try to test with our questions, whose love we try to earn with our works, silence us with a parable, humble us with a miracle! Tell us wondrous stories of Samaritans: of people who dare to touch those whom others have judged untouchable; of people who rise above long-held prejudices to kneel at the side of the wounded; of people who sacrifice time and comfort, and even pride, to save a stranger from pain.

Tell us such miraculous stories, O Christ, that our knowledge of you might increase—you who sacrificed your*self* on a criminal's cross to save your enemies. Help us to understand what you mean by *eternal life,* that we might stop trying to purchase a glorious future with righteous works. Turn our attention away from ourselves, that we might begin living eternally, *here* and *now,* showing mercy to those who are in need of mercy, even as we are shown mercy while yet unmerciful. Help us to stop abandoning to others the fate of the world while seeking privilege for ourselves; help us to begin acknowledging our responsibility to care, before the opportunity to care has passed us by.

Strengthen us in your power, Lord! It is *your* power, united with our weakness, that enables us to love someone besides ourselves. It is your power, united with our weakness, that enables us to be patient with the pain of others. It is your power, united with our weakness, that enables us to rejoice in the relief of suffering, no matter how great the cost.

We give thanks to you, O Christ, that the world has been so ordered that the power of love is the supreme power—that the power of love, even more than a faith that moves mountains, is what turns *no*bodies into *some*bodies. We praise you that what is patient and kind is superior to what is angry or cruel; that what is trusting and humble is superior to what is jealous

---

138 Litany inspired by Genesis 1.

or boastful; that what is modest and respectful is superior to what is arrogant or rude; that what can bear all things, believe all things, hope all things, and endure all things is superior to what abandons all things, doubts all things, laments all things, and concedes all things.[139]

O Lord, in the power of love we ask you: Bestow upon us a double share of your spirit. You have charged us, "If you love me, you will keep my commandments, caring for your neighbor and serving your God." You have promised us, "If you believe in me, you will do greater works than mine."[140] Dear Christ, you know that we love you; help us to love our neighbor more deeply and our God more surely. Let your spirit descend upon us, and like the Samaritan, we shall pour it out upon a suffering world, that all might be saved according to your tender mercy.

*Benediction.* May you increase in all spiritual wisdom. May you bear fruit in every good work. And may you give thanks to God—from whom you receive forgiveness, and from whom you receive the power to forgive.

## *Sunday Between July 17 and July 23 Inclusive*

*Lections:* Amos 8:1-12; Psalm 52; Colossians 1:15-28; Luke 10:38-42

*Call to Worship*
L: The mystery that was hidden for long ages has been disclosed by God—
P: Witness the Christ, in whom is hid the treasure of wisdom,[141] by whom the bread is blessed and broken.
L: The secret that was veiled for generations has been revealed by God—
P: Witness the Christ, in whom is found the wealth of forgiveness, by whom the wine is blessed and poured.

139 This paragraph inspired by I Corinthians 13:2, 4-7.
140 Inspired by John 14:15, 12.
141 Inspired by Colossians 2:2-3.

A: The time is fulfilled! The day is come! Let all in heaven
    unite with earth, singing praise to the Lord their God![142]

*Invocation.* O God, dispatch to us a prophet! Send us a saint!
Give us a healer! Show us a seer! Let them be young, or let them
be old; let them sing or dance or speak or remain silent—only
let them carry your message. For how precious are your
thoughts, O Lord! Your mysteries number more than all the
grains of sand and all the blades of grass on earth, yet all of
them are one. In *one* life we have seen them joined together,
and once having seen them, we would see them again!

Show yourself, Lord, that we might sit at your feet and listen
to your teaching!

*Litany*

L: Glory be to God, our creator!
P: How mysterious are your works, O Spirit who dwells be-
    fore us! You form all things in heaven and on earth; you
    make us one in your image.
L: Glory be to Christ, our redeemer!
P: How mysterious are your works, O God who dwells
    among us! You transform us through your cross; you
    make peace through your sacrifice.
L: Glory be to the Spirit, our sustainer!
P: How mysterious are your works, O Christ who dwells
    within us! You inform our worldly minds; you tell us
    the kingdom belongs to servants.
L: Glory be to our creator, Spirit dwelling before us!
P: How mysterious are your works, that you should also be
    forming us into *your* body, linking our members to-
    gether in your service!
L: Glory be to our redeemer, God dwelling among us!
P: How mysterious are your works, that you should also be
    transforming us into *your* servants, that we might make
    known the riches of your glory!
L: Glory be to our sustainer, Christ dwelling within us!

---

142 Inspired by Ephesians 1:9-10.

P: How mysterious are your works, that you should also be conforming us to *your* mind,[143] feeding us on milk, and then on solid food.[144]

A: O God, we praise you! For all that you have done, and all that we shall become, we give you thanks!

*Prayer for One Voice.* O Christ, you enter our community, and we receive you into our house. Sometimes, like Mary, we sit at your feet, listening to your teaching; other times, like Martha, we are distracted with much serving, and we complain that the work has been left to us alone. Then you answer us, saying, "You are anxious and troubled about many things, but only one thing is needed."

*Only one thing is needed.* How often we forget, Lord, and how often we doubt, that what you most need is not our waiting *upon* you, but our waiting *for* you—waiting for the word, through whom all things are made, and without whom nothing is done.[145] We forget; we doubt, because waiting is not easy for us. We live in a bustling world in the midst of bustling people. We have little patience and much ambition; we have little time and much talk. We fidget in silence. We squirm in idleness. We teach our children that those who say nothing have nothing to say, and that those who hesitate are lost.

O Christ, interrupt our busyness with a word about mindfulness, lest we forget the God who gives us birth. Disrupt our distractedness with a call to attention, lest we forget the Lord who provides for life. Convict us if, when we have eaten and are full, we say in our hearts, "The work of our own hands has satisfied our hunger."[146] Teach us what it means to prepare only our *daily* bread,[147] and then bless and break that loaf together in your presence, that the one loaf might multiply and feed a thousand, and then a thousand thousands.[148]

---

143 See Romans 12:2.

144 Inspired by Hebrews 5:12-14.

145 Inspired by John 1:3.

146 Inspired by Deuteronomy 32:18; 8:11-18.

147 See Matthew 6:11.

148 Inspired by Matthew 14:13-21.

Convince us, Lord, that one thing is needed for all other things; that waiting for you must come before waiting upon others. Without the word, how shall we know what is to be done, and when, and where, and how! For your word is the *why* of our deeds; it is the truth of our life!

*Many things are needed,* and many things shall be. We offer ourselves to you fully, O Christ; we are with you without reservation, without distraction. Speak to us, telling us that all things are possible if only we believe, for all things *are* possible with God. Call to us, inspiring us to the fullness of faith, for faith is nothing, if not the assurance of things hoped for and the conviction of things not seen. And charge us with the living out of the gospel, for the gospel is nothing, if not the promise of all things being made new, through our God and for our neighbor.[149]

*Benediction.* Continue steadfastly in the faith, never wavering from the hope of the gospel. Strive with all the energy that God mightily inspires within you, and remember that only one thing is needed: Love the Lord your God with all your strength, and your neighbor as yourself.

## Sunday Between July 24 and July 30 Inclusive

*Lections:* Hosea 1:2-10; Psalm 85; Colossians 2:6-15 (16-19); Luke 11:1-13

*Call to Worship*
L:  Come to the river Jordan; wash, and be made clean!
P:  Baptize us with water, and the heavens above shall open!
L:  Come to the river Jordan; shout praises to God with thanksgiving!
P:  Baptize us with water, and the Spirit shall descend!
A:  O dove, swoop down on a rushing wind; let the sound of your flight fill the house of the Lord![150]

*Invocation.* O Lord, ask whatever you will of us, and it will be given. Seek whatever you need from us, and it will be found.

---

149 See Mark 9:23; 10:27; Hebrews 11:1; Revelation 21:5.
150 Inspired by Luke 3:21-22; Acts 2:2.

Knock upon any door, and it will be opened. For while we are yet weak, we ask of you, and receive; while we are yet sinful, we seek from you, and find; and while we are yet estranged, we approach your door, and discover it open—a door none can close. Come to us, Lord, and invite us in, that we might eat at your table—you with us and we with you.[151]

*Litany*

L: Let us pray, "O God, hallowed be your name"—

P: And let us honor the name of God with works as well as with words.

L: Let us pray, "Your kingdom come, your will be done on earth as it is in heaven"—

P: And let us shake the foundations of earth in the name of heaven, that what is unshakable might remain.[152]

L: Let us pray, "Give us this day our daily bread"—

P: And let us daily break our loaves, and bless them, and share them with the crowds.

L: Let us pray, "Forgive us our debts, for we forgive everyone who sins against us"—

P: And let us love greatly, for those who love little forgive little.[153]

L: Let us pray, "Lead us not into temptation, but deliver us from evil"—

P: And let us never place a stumbling block in the way of our neighbor.[154]

L: Let us pray all these things, that our manner of life might become worthy of the gospel,

P: That we might stand firm in one spirit and strive together with one mind, all for the sake of one great love—[155]

A: For yours, O God, is the kingdom and the power and the glory forever, amen![156]

---

151 Inspired by Romans 5:6, 8, 10; Revelation 3:8, 20.
152 See Hebrews 12:27.
153 Inspired by Matthew 14:13-21; Luke 7:47.
154 See Romans 14:13.
155 See Philippians 1:27 and 2:2.
156 See also Matthew 6:9-13.

*Prayer for One Voice.* O God, whose breath stirs the trees, whose pulse moves the rivers, we praise you for your presence in our world. We can trust your presence—around us, among us, with us, with*in* us—above all else. If shades of light and dark play tricks on our eyes, we can look to you for clarity in seeing. If clamoring voices make fools of our ears, we can listen to you for clarity in hearing. If competing powers make claims on our hearts, we can turn to you for clarity in deciding. Yours is the light beside which all others are dim, the voice before which all others are faint, the power against which all others are weak.

We thank you, dear Lord, that we can take your presence for granted. But let us not take your presence lightly. Let us never forget that your presence makes two demands upon us: that we love you with all our heart and soul and mind and strength, and that we love our neighbors as ourselves—two great demands, which really are but one, like the rising and the setting sun.

Only one commandment . . . why do we have such trouble remembering, Lord? We can fill our minds daily with all kinds of facts and figures, memorize lists of names and lines of poetry, plan for a day twenty years hence or recollect a day twenty years before; but when the facts tell us that someone needs help, when the figures show that someone is in trouble, we cannot remember our responsibility, before them and before you. Forgive us, Lord, when we thus deny our baptism.

We are your people, O God. We would live in Christ! We would be rooted in the goodness of Christ, like the great forests are rooted in the good earth! Yet we are afraid, we pull back. We live in a rapidly changing world, with shifting values and uncertain loyalties. Some of us want to conquer that world with our own schemes and skills and sweat. Others of us want to retreat. Our hands, which you would stretch toward the stricken, we use to cover our ears; our eyes, which you would turn toward the unloved, we squeeze tightly shut; our mouths, with which you would proclaim release, we open to declare we won't get involved.

Convict us, Lord! Teach us that the world is not ours for us to conquer, but yours for us to tend! Convince us that we are not to retreat from the world, but return to it, filled with your compassion. Empower us, Lord! As we commit ourselves to you in this place, remind us that our commitment is meaning-less if we do not exercise it in other places. As we dedicate ourselves to you in this hour, remind us that our dedication is unacceptable if we do not express it in other hours. Let your will be our will; your kingdom, our kingdom; your power, our power; and your glory, our glory—on earth as it is in heaven, forever and ever!

*Benediction.* As once the spirit of God dwelled bodily in Jesus of Nazareth, so now the spirit of God dwells in us, the body of Christ. Being therefore members of one another, let us care for one another: If any of us suffer, let all suffer together; if any of us rejoice, let all rejoice together.[157]

## *Sunday Between July 31 and August 6 Inclusive*

*Lections:* Hosea 11:1-11; Psalm 107:1-9, 43; Colossians 3:1-11; Luke 12:13-21

*Call to Worship*
L:  Come and stand behind the Shield, the one in whom your hearts believe;
P:  Let us learn what it means to be saved by the Lord.
L:  Come and stand upon the Rock, the one on whom your hearts rely;
P:  Let us learn what it means to be strong in the Lord.
L:  Come and stand around the Shepherd, the one in whom your hearts have faith;
P:  Let us learn what it means to be loved by the Lord.
A:  O Spirit who makes us the image of God, help us become the saviors of the helpless, the pillars of the weak, the finders of the forsaken!

*Invocation.* O Spirit of God, be present with us as we gather in this place. Guide us as we seek the things that are above, that we might perceive your will for things below. Set our minds on the accomplishment of that will, that it might be done on earth as in heaven.

---

157 See I Corinthians 12:25-26.

*Litany*

L: O that all people might turn to the prophets—

P: And learn that God defines *wealth* not as the abundance of goods, but as the abundance of sharing.

L: O that all people might turn to the prophets—

P: And learn that God defines *neighbor* not by the circumstances of one's life but by the fact of one's humanity.

L: O that all people might turn to the prophets—

P: And learn that God defines *peace* not as the absence of violence but as the presence of justice.

A: O Lord, we grope like those who have no eyes, stumbling at noon as in twilight. Justice has turned back, and righteousness stands afar off; truth has fallen in the public squares, and uprightness cannot enter our towns.[158] Save us, Lord! You are the light of the world; shine upon the peoples of earth!

*Prayer for One Voice.* O Lord of the Good Harvest, receive the prayer of those who plow fields and scatter seed upon the earth, those who build barns and fill them with the fruit of their labors. We come before you humbly, asking that you enter our barns and inspect our crops. Look within us and judge whether we are rich toward you or for ourselves. Where we are found wanting, convict us, and create in us a new heart.

We confess, O Lord, that we often scatter bad seed, and the world reaps the evil we sow. We sow the seeds of anger. Sometimes the anger is ours, and we let it explode into harm—or we bury it, and allow it to fester. Sometimes we arouse anger in others, and we refuse to see it—or seeing, we refuse to address it. Forgive us, O God, when we scatter seeds of anger.

We also plant seeds of malice. We act spitefully, we act vindictively; we inflict abuse upon others, we incite violence against body and spirit. Forgive us, O God, when we scatter seeds of malice.

We acknowledge too that we spread seeds of deception. Our words cannot be trusted, our works cannot be taken at face value. We consider sincerity a sign of naiveté; we regard integ-

---

158 Inspired by Isaiah 59:9-14.

rity as old-fashioned. Forgive us, O God, when we scatter seeds of deception.

Our barns are full, O Lord, but they are bursting with bitter fruits. Where we keep anger, you would have stored compassion; where we keep malice, you would have stored love; where we keep deception, you would have stored truth. Compassion, love, truth: These and more you would have us sow and reap, increase and multiply, that all might eat and be filled, drink and be satisfied, make merry and be thankful, being rich toward you, the Provider of Life.

Destroy the bad seed within us, Lord. Burn our dross with the purifying fire, and make room for new seeds, new works, new harvests. Help us to plant your seeds and tend your fields, and the mustard trees of your realm will flourish, fed by the waters of justice rolling down your holy mountain.

*Benediction.* Do not lay up for yourselves treasures on earth, where moth and rust consume and thieves break in and steal, but lay up for yourselves treasures in heaven. Bury yourselves with Christ in God, that you might arise in the glory of Christ's love for the world. Let the love of Christ be the measure of your wealth, for where your heart is, there shall your treasure be also.[159]

## Sunday Between August 7 and August 13 Inclusive

*Lections:* Isaiah 1:1, 10-20; Psalm 50:1-8, 22-23; Hebrews 11:1-3, 8-19; Luke 12:32-40

### Call to Worship

L: Come now, says the Lord, let us reason together,

P: That our sins, though they be like scarlet, may be white as snow.

L: Let us give ear to the teaching of our God,

P: That we may be shaped into vessels of mercy.[160]

L: Lord, you are the potter, and we are the clay;[161]

---

159 Inspired by Matthew 6:19-21.

160 Inspired by Romans 9:22-23.

161 See Isaiah 64:8.

P: "Mold us and make us after your will, while we are waiting, yielded and still."[162]

*Invocation.* O God, when you hear some of us utter, "There is no God!" you must be amazed that those fashioned by your own hands should contend, "No one has made us!"[163] And when others of us rebel, trampling your courts, you must be astounded that those made in your own image should complain, "Creation is flawed!"[164]

Do not despair of us, Lord, but renew our faith. If faith be the assurance of things hoped for, reassure us! If faith be the conviction of things not seen, convince us! Remake us, firmly yet gently, that we might cease doubting you and degrading ourselves!

*Litany*

L: O people, prepare!
P: Awake, O world, and watch!
L: Let your light burn throughout the night,
P: And keep your vigil throughout the day;
L: For Christ is coming at any time—
P: The hour no one knows.[165]
L: Behold, Christ will stand at our door and knock—
P: A man who is hungry, a woman who is thirsty,
L: A stranger who is lonely, a child who is cold,
P: A neighbor who is sick, a person who is lost;[166]—
L: Whatever the face, let us hear the voice,
P: And open the door at once![167]
L: Whatever is asked, let Christ be given;
P: Whatever is sought, let Christ receive;[168]
L: O people, prepare!
P: Awake, O world, and watch!
A: Whenever the knock, let Christ come in!

---

162 From Adelaide A. Pollard, "Have Thine Own Way, Lord."
163 See Isaiah 29:16.
164 Inspired by Isaiah 45:9.
165 See Matthew 24:36.
166 Inspired by Matthew 25:31-46.
167 See Revelation 3:20.
168 Inspired by Luke 11:9

*Prayer for One Voice.* O God, who confronts us with hopeful tomorrows, despite our rebellious yesterdays, we approach you in gratitude. We put ourselves in your hands, though our sins be like scarlet, assured that you can take all that is wrong with us and make it right, that you can take all that is good about us and make it better.

We do not sing about "amazing grace" simply because a hymn writer has composed the lines. We sing about it because your grace at work in our life has never ceased to amaze us. We marvel at its power to transplant and to transform. Your grace turned Abraham and Sarah from comfortable residents of a reputable city into tent-dwelling but happy nomads; your grace turned Moses from a stammering youth into an eloquent liberator; your grace turned Ruth from an obscure widow into a determined heroine; your grace turned Isaiah from a preacher of judgment into a proclaimer of forgiveness; your grace turned Mary from a scorned refugee into a keeper of divine secrets; your grace turned Saul, a fierce persecutor of Christians, into Paul, a forceful proclaimer of Christian faith.

Your grace at work in human life is no less amazing today. "The old, old story" can be repeated, if only we can transcend our past: a past when we were less circumspect about the places we frequented; less careful about the power we wielded; less scrupulous about the money we spent; less concerned about the practices we encouraged. O Lord, release us from our past, that we might experience the freedom for which Christ set us free, and serve one another in love.

We do not pray for ourselves alone. We pray for all whose tomorrows are overcast with the shadows of their yesterdays. Blot out their painful memories, and deliver us from the temptation to rekindle their pain. Let us remember that you do not appoint us either as judges over them or as keepers of their conscience. You *do* appoint us to open the door when they knock, that they might come in and sup with you, and you with them.

We thank you, dear Lord, that your amazing grace still abounds, and that, just as you made our ancestors its channel for us, you make us its channel for others. If there be in us any obstacle to its flow, we pray that you will not let it remain. Remove it far from us, so that in days to come, when your people sing "Amaz-

139

ing Grace," they will praise you—not as the God of the past but as the God of the present; not as the God who was but as the God who *is*—is now, and evermore shall be.

*Benediction.* As God sends us from this place, let us go forth in the faith that led Abraham and Sarah toward a new world. Let us, like them, refuse ever to turn back, that the day might soon dawn when our works of faith shall be as countless as the stars in the heavens and the grains of sand on the seashore.

## Sunday Between August 14 and August 20 Inclusive

*Lections:* Isaiah 5:1-7; Psalm 80:1-2, 8-19; Hebrews 11:29–12:2; Luke 12:49-56

*Call to Worship*
L:   Sing to God! Praise the Lord!
P:   The afflicted are not forgotten; the weak are not forsaken!
L:   Sing to God! Praise the Lord!
P:   The obedient are not neglected; the faithful are not abandoned!
A:   As smoke is swept away by wind, as wax is melted down before fire, wickedness perishes before the Lord! O let the world be jubilant with joy; O let us exalt before our God![169]

*Invocation.* O God, you have cast fire upon the earth; its heat sears our troubled conscience. We are weary with running from its flames—we can run no longer. O Lord, let them consume every sin that clings closely to us, that to you we may commit our cause and entrust our life! With all our hearts we seek you—baptize us with your presence!

*Litany*
L:   Christ came to cast fire upon the earth;
P:   Would that it were already kindled!
L:   The day approaches—it burns like an oven:
P:   Our pride and our evil will soon become as stubble;
L:   Sparks will be struck on the rock of God,
P:   And red flames will dance in the dark of the night.

---

169 Inspired by Psalm 68:2-3.

L:   The day approaches—it flashes like lightning:
P:   Our weapons of war will soon blaze in a heap;
L:   Streaks will fork down from the finger of God,
P:   And the flames will rage for seven long years.[170]
L:   The day approaches—it scorches like the sun:
P:   Our idols will soon be pitched in the fire;[171]
L:   Light will stream down from the eye of God,
P:   And the gods will die in the dust of their ashes.
L:   O Christ, cast down your fire upon the earth;
P:   Would that it were already kindled!

*Prayer for One Voice.* O God of endless surprises, who chastens us when we look for comfort and comforts us when we look for chastening, who challenges us when we expect to be praised and praises us when we expect to be challenged, you are the Lord our God, the one before whom we bow in fear and trembling, in adoration and praise. Sometimes we would prefer that you be a little more predictable and not quite so full of surprises! If only your ways were not so different from ours and your thoughts so much higher than ours! Then we could come before you in confidence and pride. But we would not know who should be praying to whom. So we thank you, dear Lord, for your frequent reminders of the distance between you and ourselves.

We wish we could do without these reminders, but daily we prove our need for them. We sound warnings of your judgment, and when it does not strike, we doubt not our knowledge, but your power. We call for the destruction of our enemies, and when they are not destroyed, we question not our righteousness, but your justice. We seek places of honor, and when others obtain them, we indict not our ambition, but your faithfulness. We pray for peace with justice, and when we must settle for injustice without peace, we question not our passion, but your commitment. Not only do we hold you responsible for the wrongs we do. We also hold you responsible for the wrongs *we* could *undo*—if only instead of looking up for the

---

170 Inspired by Malachi 4:1; Psalm 46:9; Ezekiel 39:9-10.
171 See Isaiah 37:19.

problem, we would look within; if only instead of looking within for the solution, we would look up.

Forgive us, O God, for the shameful way we exonerate ourselves at your expense. We blame you for things for which we are responsible, and we praise ourselves for things for which you are responsible. We are quick to indict those who frustrate our quest for fulfillment, and slow to credit those who advance it. Yet a cloud of your witnesses surrounds us. They are those who look not to Washington or Wall Street for guidance, but to the prophets and apostles; who slay the dragon of personal greed on the altar of human service; who risk failure for the sake of honesty rather than seek advantage through dishonesty; who measure success not by the speed with which they move up but by the grace with which they reach out. If we have yet to catch a glimpse of these people, open our eyes, dear Lord. Forgive us for allowing our sight to become so distorted that we no longer can separate the wheat from the chaff.

Open our eyes, O Lord, that we might behold among us those who incarnate the spirit of the one who incarnated your spirit. Open our imaginations, that we might behold within us another candidate for the incarnation of that same spirit. And open our hearts, that we might behold around us still others who are anxious to receive your grace. They are ready and waiting. Help us, dear Lord, to make sure they must wait no longer.

*Benediction*

L: May God lift up each sagging shoulder and strengthen every weakened knee;
P: May God straighten the path for each tired foot and turn to peace every embattled heart;
L: May God so bless each merciful word and magnify every faithful deed,
A: That each root of bitterness can be pulled from the earth and the tree of life planted in its place.

*Sunday Between August 21 and August 27 Inclusive*

*Lections:* Jeremiah 1:4-10; Psalm 71:1-6; Hebrews 12:18-29; Luke 13:10-17

*Call to Worship*

L: Come, let us seek rest at the altar of God—

P: Where even the infant can find comfort and protection; where even the weak can find peace and justice.

L: Blessed are they who dwell in God's presence—

P: Where even the lily may grow in glory, where even the grass may be clothed with life.[172]

A: Blessed are they who trust in you, O Lord, our Home and our Provider!

*Invocation.* How lovely is the city of our God! In it are many dwelling places,[173] and within them is what no eye has ever seen, no ear has ever heard, no heart has ever dreamed. Anxious that every room be filled, you, O God, send your servants into the streets of the city and the roads of the country, and they bring us in—the poor, the maimed, the blind, the lame. And still there is room! Now, O Lord, inspire us to carry your presence to those who have been left alone, that all might dwell in your city forever![174]

*Litany*

L: O God, you speak from a burning bush, and the bush is not consumed;

P: Is this what it means to be baptized with fire? O Lord, we stand on your holy ground, frightened by your mystery!

L: You speak from the dazzling light on the road, and we can see nothing for days;[175]

P: Is this what it means to be blind, yet have eyes?[176] O Lord, we kneel on your strange highway, frightened by your mystery!

L: You speak from the whirlwind,[177] so loud that we stop our ears with our fingers;

---

172 See Matthew 6:26-30.

173 See John 14:2.

174 Inspired by I Corinthians 2:9; Luke 14:22-23; Psalm 23:6.

175 Inspired by Exodus 3:1-6; Matthew 3:11; Acts 9:3-9.

176 See Isaiah 43:8.

177 Inspired by Job 38:1.

P: Is this what it means to have ears, yet not hear? O Lord, we shrink from your sacred tempest, frightened by your mystery!

L: You speak from the height of the highest mountain, and the mountain becomes a lowly plain;

P: Is this what it means to be shaken, that foundations of sand may fall? O Lord, we hug your hallowed earth, frightened by your mystery!

L: O God, grant us the powers you give to prophets, to understand riddles and tongues and knowledge—

P: Cast out our fear with the fullness of your love, the mystery that neither fades nor passes away![178]

*Prayer for One Voice.* O gracious God, to whose greatness our worship adds nothing, but without whose worship we diminish everything, we lift our hearts and voices in gratitude for the opportunity of worship; for this place in which to render worship; and for the church of Jesus Christ, whose spirit always informs our worship—and sometimes inspires us to *reform* our worship.

We are grateful for your prophets, who shine the light of your judgment into the dark corners of our lives. At the time, we may not know that it costs them as much pain to expose us as it costs us to be exposed. But the fact of their pain dawns upon us, once we heed their rebuke and see that their joy is as great as ours. O God, we thank you for these truth-sayers, without whom we truth-seekers might substitute our camaraderie with one another for communion with you. If we are troubled by the presence of your prophets, let us ask ourselves if we have not become too comfortable in *your* presence. Help us to realize that the only thing we need fear from the prophets is their absence or, worse, a church in which they are silenced.

We confess, O Lord, that this lesson is not an easy one. Often, when persons speak to us in your name, we listen not to those who confront us with your judgment, but to those who console us with your favor; not to those who highlight our responsibilities, but to those who keynote our privileges; not to those

179 Inspired by Matthew 7:24-27; I Corinthians 13.

who stress our equality with others, but to those who emphasize our superiority. We wish we could blame your misguided prophets for our betrayal of you, but we know our deceitful hearts give wings to deceitful tongues.

Forgive us, dear God, for our selfishness of heart: the selfishness that makes us insensitive to your word, indifferent to your messengers, and unfaithful to your mission. Renew our appreciation for the church as the body of Christ, and for ourselves as its members, open to your guidance and committed to your service. As Christ has opened the door of your kingdom to all your children, let us open the doors of his church to all your children, that his unanswered prayer that we become one—even as you and he are one—might be answered in our lifetime.

O God, even as we lament the divisions that afflict your church, let us labor to heal the divisions that plague your world. Let not the Christians in lands of persecution and poverty be forgotten in lands of peace and plenty. Give to your church a mind quick to sense the needs of all its members; a heart able to feel their pain; and a hand ready to offer the help for which they long. Make the church, like the Christ to whom it bears witness, a beacon for all humanity.

*Benediction.* Christ our brother has proclaimed a feast in the city of the living God. Let us gather together from all corners of the earth—a multitude without number, from all nations and tribes and peoples and tongues; and let us prepare a place for one another at the Lord's table, where none shall ever fear or hunger or thirst again.[179]

## Sunday Between August 28 and September 3 Inclusive

*Lections:* Jeremiah 2:4-13; Psalm 81:1, 10-16; Hebrews 13:1-8, 15-16; Luke 14:1, 7-14

*Call to Worship*
L:  Who shall shout for joy to the Lord our God?
P:  Who shall find refuge in the arms of our God?

---

179 See Revelation 7:9, 16.

L: They who hear and heed the voice of the Lord;
P: They who learn and walk in the ways of the Lord.
L: From the love of God they shall never be separated—
P: Though they travel the world, they shall not be alone!

*Invocation.* Yesterday and today and forever, all the peoples are yours, O Lord. As one day in your sight is a thousand years,[180] so one life in your sight is a multitude.

O God, be present with *us,* as you are with all; be present *now,* as you are forever. To you we offer ourselves, as individuals and as a body; to you we open ourselves, this and every day.

*Litany*

L: The hand of the Lord has touched your lips, putting God's word in your mouth.[181] What have you heard with the ears of your heart? What are you sent to proclaim?
W: The word of the Lord has come to us, saying, "My people have indicted me, charging that I have forsaken them;
M: "To this I reply, in anger and sorrow: Is it not *you* who have forsaken me?—
W: "You, who approach me with prayers on your lips, while your wandering spirits are far away;[182]
M: "You, who do wrong under cover of night, thinking, 'Who will be out and about now to see?'[183]
W: "You, who make plans, though the plans are not mine;[184]
M: "You, who do good—for those who repay?
W: "Despite your sin, you judge the world and declare that you are innocent,
M: "And your pride digs a canyon between earth and heaven, accusing *your God* of guilt and transgression!
W: "Can you not see what a horrible thing is happening upon the earth?
M: "Your prophets prophesy falsely, and your people heed their words;

---

180 See II Peter 3:8.
181 Inspired by Jeremiah 1:9.
182 See Isaiah 29:13.
183 Inspired by Isaiah 29:15.
184 See Isaiah 30:1.

W: "Your leaders take you down terrible paths,[185] and you are content to follow!

M: "Tell me, you stubborn and rebellious people: What will you do when the end comes?

A: *"Yes, what will you do in the end?"*[186]

*Prayer for One Voice.* O Lord of love, who instructs us in all the ways we can be taught, and who seeks us in all the ways we can be found, you are our Teacher, without whose instruction we would be constantly confused; and our Guide, without whose companionship we would daily go astray. We thank you for your generosity, for your readiness so freely and fully to teach us and to lead us.

We thank you, too, that you were equally generous to our ancestors, while always careful to adapt your presence to their need, just as you do to ours. Not only did you give them the law for shaping their life, but you gave them your love for reshaping their law. Let us not mistake your guidance and instruction of them for your guidance and instruction of us. But let us deal justly and gently with our ancestors, learning from their mistakes and profiting from their insights.

We must confess, O God, that we have been slow to do so. While our ancestors asserted the power of grace to beget goodness, we withhold the offer of grace until we behold the evidence of goodness. While they encouraged hospitality to strangers, we act as strangers even toward our neighbors. While they remembered those in prison as if imprisoned with them, we shun prisoners as if they were not human beings. While they steeled themselves against love of money, we pursue riches as if they were all that mattered. While they felt the pain of injustice as if its victims, we leave the campaign for justice to others.

O God, help us to realize that if we do not walk in your ways, it is not always because our ancestors have neglected to teach your word. As often as not, it is because we have ignored their wise counsel and good example. The fault lies not with pre-

185 Inspired by Jeremiah 2:34-35; Isaiah 59:2; 9:16.
186 See Jeremiah 5:30-31.

147

vious generations, but with ours. Those in need of forgiveness are neither the people who came before us nor the people who live around us, but ourselves.

Forgive us, dear God, for denying our responsibility for the world in which we dwell. Grant us the grace neither to blame our ancestors for our mistakes nor to rob our descendants of their birthright. Help us to bequeath to them a world that will respect their dignity and honor their dreams—a world that will nurture body, mind, and spirit, with privilege for all and prejudice for none.

O Lord, bless the ties that bind us to those who have gone before and to those who shall come after. We pray for wisdom, lest we become so obsessed with yesterday's mistakes that we hesitate to seize today's opportunities; and we pray for courage, lest we become so despondent over our failure to make the world perfect that we stop trying to make it better. Help us to demand of ourselves neither more nor less than we demand of our ancestors and descendants. Let us acknowledge the members of all generations as our sisters and brothers in your family, that we might honor you by honoring them.

*Benediction.* Let our love for one another continue. Let us not love ourselves only, but show compassion also to strangers, for thereby we may entertain angels unawares.

### Sunday Between September 4 and September 10 Inclusive

*Lections:* Jeremiah 18:1-11; Psalm 139:1-6, 13-18; Philemon 1-21; Luke 14:25-33

*Call to Worship*
L: Once we were slaves, and God's word came upon us;
P: Now we are free in the Lord!
L: Once we were freeborn, and God's word fell upon us;
P: Now we are bound to the Lord!
L: Let us not return to the chains of the world,
P: But rejoice in our freedom, bought at such a great price!
L: Let us not break the fetters of the Lord,

P:  But give thanks for our yoke, forged by such a great love![187]

*Invocation.* O Christ, when our sins are fashioned into a yoke and set upon our necks, when our transgressions are tied together and laid upon our shoulders,[188] with the strength of your arm you break the yoke and lift away the burden.[189]

Come to us, O Lord, for we have come to you, laboring and heavy-laden.[190] Give us rest, and teach us to be gentle and lowly in heart, that we might learn to wear the yoke that is easy and to bear the burden that is light.

*Litany*

L:  O see how the vessel spoils in the potter's hand!

P:  Can the Lord not do the same with us? God's trumpet blares above the tumult—we hear and tremble.[191]

L:  The Lord has come upon me, saying, "Mortal, be my mouthpiece! Speak my word like a mighty horn, and declare to my people their sins!"[192]

P:  Your trumpet is silver, but its sound is harsh!

L:  Hearken to its call! The Lord asks, "Why have your hands not released the oppressed? Why have you not broken every yoke and chain?"

P:  Tell the Lord that we have no power.

L:  Hear the trumpet! "Why have you not shared bread with the hungry? Why have you not found shelter for the homeless?"

P:  Tell the Lord that we have no time.

L:  The trumpet cries! "Why do you leave the naked uncovered? Why do you neglect a neighbor in pain?"[193]

P:  Tell the Lord—we have no excuse.

---

187 See I Corinthians 7:22-23.

188 See Lamentations 1:14.

189 Inspired by Isaiah 9:4; 10:27.

190 See Matthew 11:28-30.

191 Inspired by Exodus 19:16.

192 See Isaiah 58:1.

193 Inspired by Numbers 10:21; Isaiah 58:6; 58:7.

L: I've seen suffering coming upon the land; I've blown the Lord's trumpet in warning! Now who will rise for God against evil? Who will stand for God against sin?

P: Put a trumpet into *our* hands, and we will blow for the Lord!

L: Raise the Lord's cause with its holy sound! Split the air with its righteous peal—

A: Let us march to the trumpet of jubilee,[194] proclaiming liberty throughout the land! The world will hear, and all the nations will shout, and the walls that divide us will come tumbling down![195]

*Prayer for One Voice.* O Christ, revealer of God to us and of us to God, you are unlike anything, unlike any*one* we have ever known, eternally faithful to God and infinitely faithful to God's people. Yet you risk everything, entrusting us with the work of your holy realm, just as God has entrusted us with the stewardship of the natural world. You ask that we be filled with your spirit, that we become like you—you, whose consolations cheer our souls when the cares of our hearts are too many; you, whose dreams inspire our souls when the burdens on our hearts are too heavy; you, whose words enlighten our souls when the eyes of our hearts are too blind; you, whose deeds humble our souls when the intentions of our hearts are too proud. How you honor us, Lord! And how we would honor you!

How gracious you are! Though you have the authority and the power simply to command us to do whatever you need us to do, yet for love's sake, you *appeal* to us, that we might *choose* to do good, freely and not by compulsion. How gracious you are, that you do not just overwhelm us with what you require— that instead, you invite us to unite our will with yours! How you honor us, Lord! And how we would honor you!

Yet we are tempted to keep you at a safe distance, so that when you call, we can pretend not to hear; when you point to where we are needed, we can seem preoccupied; when you grip our arm, we can pull away. As if you might tire of troubling us with tasks we don't want, and turn to someone else for help—someone with more time, more money, more

---

194 See Judges 7:16, 18; Leviticus 25:8-9.

195 Inspired by Joshua 6:5.

power, more personality, more talent, more status, more reason, more *something!* We *do* admire what you desire, Lord, but even we know that admiration is not devotion. Devotion is far more costly, and we are not sure we really want to pay that cost. Devotion is the bearing of a cross, and we are not sure we really want to carry that cross.

O Christ, forgive us for seeking far more from you than we are willing to give in return—not only to you, but to all those to whom you would have us give. Fill our hearts with an unwavering resolve and an unceasing love. Help us to be unlike anyone we have ever known—anyone except you; make us eternally faithful to you and infinitely faithful to your people. Help us to risk everything as we labor in your vineyard and care for the world. Refresh us with your spirit, that we might cheer our neighbors when the cares of their hearts are too many; inspire them when the burdens on their hearts are too heavy; enlighten them when the eyes of their hearts are too blind; and humble them when the intentions of their hearts are too proud.

We pray these things out of the greatness and the smallness of our faith—a faith given not to this world, but to the world that is to come.

*Benediction.* May the God of grace create in you that which is pleasing in the Lord's sight; and may the God of peace equip you with everything good to do the Lord's will.

## Sunday Between September 11 and September 17 Inclusive

*Lections:* Jeremiah 4:11-12, 22-28; Psalm 14; I Timothy 1:12-17; Luke 15:1-10

### Call to Worship
L: Are you the lamb for whom the shepherd left the other ninety-and-nine; who, having been found, was the cause of great rejoicing?
P: We are the lamb who went astray. Let there be joy on earth as in heaven!
L: Are you the coin for which the woman lit the lamp and searched the house; which, having been found, was the cause of much celebration?

151

P:  We are the coin that was lost from the ten. Let us, with angels, sing glory to God!

*Invocation.* O Christ, who was crucified for breaking bread with sinners, welcome us into your presence. We are the foremost among sinners, but having blasphemed your name, now we would bless it; having persecuted your spirit, now we would receive it. We come before you seeking mercy; we kneel before you asking forgiveness. Let your grace overflow upon us, that we might be filled with your faith and love. To you, the immortal, invisible Christ of God, we humbly give honor and glory, forever and ever.

*Litany*

L:  What god is like our God?
P:  What other god desires not ritual but righteousness—
L:  Not ceremony but service—
P:  Not words but works?
L:  What god's love is like the love of our God?
P:  What other god wants not obedience but oneness—
L:  Not conformity but communion—
P:  Not compliance but creativity?
L:  What god's face is like the face of our God?
P:  What other god looks not *away* from us but *toward* us—
L:  Not *down* upon us but *with* us—
P:  Not *through* us but *into* us?
L:  The Lord our God is holy: There *is* no god like our God.
A:  Let us return to the Holy One: Our world is stricken, but God will heal us; our world is torn, but God will bind us up; our world is lost, but God will find us; our world is crucified, but God will raise us up!

*Prayer for One Voice:* O Lord, the mountains tremble and the clouds pour forth rain; the skies thunder, and lightning flashes on every side. Your voice is in the whirlwind, and your path is through the waters that roar and foam—yours is a broad and mighty road, yet your footprints are unseen! You come and go, and though you never really leave us, you never really show yourself, either. Miracles, wonders, signs: These are small things to which we cling, as if they somehow document your faithfulness. We cling to them steadfastly, although time and again you warn us not to erect our house of faith upon them, lest it collapse in a storm like a house built upon sand.[196]

Temptation is powerful, Lord. We ignore your warning. We shore up our faith by construing our success as proof of your faithfulness: We interpret our prosperity as your blessing, our good fortune as your favor, a turn of luck as your sign of approval, a lack of resistance as your sanction. We are so intent upon earning your love for ourselves that our neighbors are soon left unnoticed, unseen, unheard, misunderstood, mistreated.

So now you have a quarrel with us, Lord. And we are surprised, but without cause. You have watched in open-mouthed astonishment as we turned away from one another, thinking that we were turning toward you. You have watched as faithfulness has faded from the land, as kindness fell victim to neglect, as trust was strained and broken. You have watched us walk in and out of church, offering you tithes while withholding our lives, and you have been amazed that we did not hear the grieving of creation. We did not pay attention to her sorrow; her beasts in the field, her birds in the air, her fish in the sea—they vanished. The fruits of the trees rotted, the crops in the fields were choked by weeds. Our toil turned empty, our art became a lament, our eyes scrutinized every person we met, and we wondered: Is he my enemy? Is she my competition? In all the land no one asks: Isn't he my brother? Isn't she my sister? Isn't that little one my child? Isn't that elder one my parent?

Help us, Lord! Forgive us, for we have sinned! You desire us to know you; we have tried to *win* you. You desire love; we have given liturgy. You desire justice; we have sung a song. You desire righteousness; we have planned solemn assemblies.[197]

O God, show us your face! Show us a face whose eyes dream of justice, that the same dream might burn in our eyes. Show us a face whose mouth proclaims the love of kindness, that the same proclamation might issue from our mouths.[198] What do you require of us but to walk humbly with you and our neighbors?

---

196 Inspired by Psalm 46:3; Matthew 7:24-27.

197 Inspired by Amos 5:21-24.

198 Inspired by Micah 6:8.

Revive us! Raise us up! Give us strength! For there is so much that must be done, and so much that must be undone.

O Lord, let the mountains tremble, and we shall embrace those who tremble with them. Let the clouds pour forth their rain, and we shall carry the water to the thirsty. Let the skies thunder, and we shall open the ears of the deaf. Let lightning flash on every side, and we shall heal the eyes of the blind. Miracles, wonders, signs: These are the things that we shall do for your children out of the abundance of faithfulness. We shall cling steadfastly—not to what we *do*, but to who our neighbors are, and to who we are when we are with them. Help us to build our house upon love, for we know that a house built upon love will stand firm in the fullness of your presence, even as a house built upon rock.[199]

*Benediction.* Let not our love for one another be like a hot wind blowing out of the bare heights of the desert. Let it be like a spring whose waters never fail, pouring forth from the fountain of God.[200]

## Sunday Between September 18 and September 24 Inclusive

*Lections:* Jeremiah 8:18–9:1; Psalm 79:1-9; I Timothy 2:1-7; Luke 16:1-13

### Call to Worship
L: Fear not, O my people, for God shall redeem you from trouble!
P: We have spoken words reeking with risk, but the Lord shall make us stand strong against temptation.
L: Fear not, O my people, for God shall redeem you from trouble!
P: We have spent hours burdened with distress, but the Lord shall make us wax confident amidst turmoil.
L: Fear not, O my people, for God shall redeem you from trouble!
P: We have traveled paths live with danger, but the Lord shall make us lie down in safety.

---

199 Inspired by Matthew 7:24-27.
200 See Isaiah 58:11; Revelation 21:6.

L: Fear not, O my people, for God shall redeem you from trouble!
P: We have cried tears dripping with guilt, but the Lord shall make us go forth with joy!

*Invocation.* O Lord, we have not dealt as faithfully with you as you have with us. We promised to serve no god but you, but we have erected graven images in our hearts, if not on our altars. We vowed to honor your name, but we have taken it in vain. So now we pray that you will grant us the knowledge that there is a balm in Gilead, and also the grace to apply it to ourselves.

Teach us to live in faith, Lord. Make us sure of your love for us, make us unwavering in our love for you. Then, when we stumble upon the road, we will have the will to get up again and continue our journey toward the rising sun.

*Litany*
L: One who is steadfast in little will be steadfast in much,
P: And one who is dishonest in little will be dishonest in much.
L: Therefore, let us shun every way that is false,
P: And let us seek the way that is faithful;
L: Let our lips pronounce mammon unbefitting of our trust—
P: And let our lives prove more worthy of God's.
L: Let us spurn all temptations to justify greed,
P: And spread, instead, a wealth of true riches:
L: The coins of kindness and mercy and patience;
P: The fortunes of grace, which God lavishes on all;[201]
L: The treasures of wisdom and knowledge and strength,
P: Which, hidden in Christ, must be unearthed for the world.[202]
L: Let us be faithful to one god alone,
P: And let that one be the Lord our Savior—
L: Lest, serving many gods, we despise neighbor and Maker;
A: Lest, serving many gods, we despise ourselves!

*Prayer for One Voice.* O Lord, our Lord, you are the salve of the soul: Hear our supplications! The soul of our world is weary,

---

201 See Romans 2:4; Ephesians 1:7-8.
202 Inspired by Colossians 2:2-3.

needing your balm. Its past is a burden on our shoulders; its present is a stumbling block before our feet; its tomorrow is lost in a vast maze, for which we can find no map. Everything is shifting, changing so fast that the very earth trembles. We lose our footing and fall, only to be dragged along the ground by some unseen hand that will not let us go. We are frightened, Lord. Sometimes we feel weak and helpless; sometimes we feel angry and powerless. So we have returned to you, the Faithful One, our Help in time of trouble. We return to you and ask for courage. We return to you and ask for wisdom.

O Lord, our Lord, you are the prophecy of the spirit: Hear our prayers! The spirit of our world is torn, needing your voice. Its lands are rent by war and wrong; its peoples are divided by color and creed and class and culture; its unity is ripped into a million shreds, and we can find no pattern by which to mend. Everything is straining, pulling apart so hard that the very earth groans. We yearn for a word, Lord. Sometimes we feel ignorant and foolish; sometimes we feel overwhelmed and defenseless. So we have returned to you, the Faithful One, our Voice in time of trouble. We return to you and ask for judgment. We return to you and ask for clarity.

O Lord, our Lord, you are the inner movings of the heart: Hear our intercessions! The heart of our world is indifferent, needing your stimulation. Its eyes refuse to look upon the suffering; its ears refuse to listen to the abused; its lips refuse to speak out for the oppressed. Everything is numb, paralyzed so deeply that the very earth sleeps. Stir us awake, Lord. Sometimes we feel dead and listless; sometimes we feel cut off and hopeless. So we have returned to you, the Faithful One, our Inspiration in time of trouble. We return to you and ask for revival. We return to you and ask for resurrection.

O Lord, our Lord, you are the thoughts of the mind: Hear our thanksgivings! The mind of our world is confused, needing your counsel, and we trust that you will grant understanding. If its intentions are not honorable; if its ambitions are not just; if its aspirations are not fair; if everything is muddled, so clouded that the very earth doubts its turning on its axis, we believe that you will make things plain. If we feel bewildered and aimless; if we feel defeated and hapless, you will give direction. For this we have returned to you, the Faithful One, our Hope in time of trouble. We have returned to ask for your salvation; we have returned to ask for your presence; and we know that we shall receive.

*Benediction*
L: We came in faith, though the way was slow;
P: We leave in faith, with wings on our heels.
L: We came trusting God, though the road was hard;
P: We leave trusting God, with dreams in our hearts.
L: Let us go in joy, for God has traced our paths in the dust of the earth;
P: And let us return in joy, that our paths might meet forever in the spirit of this place.

## Sunday Between September 25 and October 1 Inclusive

*Lections:* Jeremiah 32:1-3*a*, 6-15; Psalm 91:1-6, 14-16; I Timothy 6:6-19; Luke 16:19-31

*Call to Worship*
L: O people, approach the Unapproachable; stand radiant in its splendor, and become children of the Light![203]
P: Let us love one another, for they who love one another abide in the Light,[204] and do not lose their way.
L: O people, enter into the Eternal; stand radiant in its glory, and become children of the Day!
P: Let us love the Lord, for they who love the Lord dwell in the Light of Day, and have no need for night.[205]

*Invocation.* O God, you promised to protect those who know your name; Lord, we know your name! You promised to answer those who call upon you; Lord, we call upon you! You promised to deliver those who love you; Lord, we love you! Pour out your spirit, that we might know that you are in our midst—that you are our God, and shall not be moved![206]

---

203 Inspired by Psalm 34:5; Ephesians 5:8.
204 See I John 2:10.
205 Inspired by I Thessalonians 5:5; Revelation 21:22-23.
206 Inspired by Psalm 46:5.

*Litany*

L:  O Christ, who suffers the wounds inflicted by sin, forgive
    your people, who have sinned against you.
P:  We have turned rushing rivers into empty desert and
    flowing springs into thirsty ground; we have reduced a
    promised land to a salty waste, a fruitful land to a bar-
    ren desert.
L:  Forgive us, Lord, who have taken your life.
P:  We have sent hurting neighbors to a far place, and trou-
    bled friends a safe distance away; we have redefined
    *neighbors* as they who do good, and redefined *friends* as
    they who need little.
L:  Forgive us, Lord, who have taken your life.
P:  O Christ, who suffers the wounds inflicted by sin, redeem
    your people, who have sinned against earth.
L:  Help us, Lord, who would restore your life.
P:  We would fill the desert with pools of water and return
    its sands to fertile ground; we would remake the waste-
    land into a sacred garden and refashion the wilderness
    into a holy place.
L:  Help us, Lord, who would restore your life.
P:  We would bring all people into our care and relieve their
    hurt and trouble; we would respect as "neighbor" each
    one who lives, and respect as "friend" each yet to be born.
A:  O Lord, our sinful hearts have been pierced, as was your
    crucified side; let our hearts be restored, as was your
    life, that we might raise your earth from the dead!

*Prayer for One Voice.* O God, you cross back and forth across the
earth to recover all who are lost in oppression and sorrow. And
you pour contempt upon the tormentors of their bodies and
souls, causing them to wander in trackless wastes until they
perceive the error of their ways. We praise you for raising up
those who are needy and afflicted and for bringing low those
who magnify their need and affliction. We praise you with
hopeful and with penitent hearts, for we have been both the
persecuted you save and the persecutors you scorn.

You know even better than we, O Lord, that we have lived
on both sides of the great and growing chasm that separates

those who have enough from those who do not—that deep and deepening gulf between those who feast sumptuously every day and those who, like Lazarus, lie outside the gate, fed only with scraps from the others' table. We confess that when we hear the parable of the rich person and Lazarus, we identify with the suffering one, wishing we could receive more compassion and be relieved of our pain, in this life as in the next. We *have* experienced great pain, Lord, and we are grateful that you are willing to enter our lives to transform that pain; that you reach to embrace us with the caring arms of friends and family, or perhaps even a stranger; that you seek to save us by whatever means your spirit can inspire. You do, indeed, come to us in the desert.

But, Lord, too often we aspire to be the wealthy. We desire to have more than we have, even when more would be too much. Our desire grows like an insatiable appetite and leads us into temptation. Our feet become ensnared in traps we set for others, or in traps we did not mean to set at all. Our senseless ambitions plunge even innocent people into pain and ruin. Watching, scheming, pinching, planning, we eventually cannot stand the misery, and we seek some way to escape it.

Great and saving God, convict us: Show us how grievous a sin it is to set our hopes on uncertain riches. Teach us to rest our lives on you, who so richly provides for us, and who would have us so faithfully provide for others. Help us to do good, to become rich in the compassion of liberal hearts and generous hands. We are your workers; direct us in our labor. Show us how to close the chasm that cuts any one of us off from the rest of us, that every rich one might join hands with every Lazarus, that all of us might take hold of the life that is life indeed.

*Benediction.* O people of God, aim at righteousness, and shun iniquity; aim at steadfastness, and shun disloyalty; aim at gentleness, and shun cruelty; aim at faithfulness, and shun hypocrisy; but most of all, aim at love, and *shun no one.*

### Sunday Between October 2 and October 8 Inclusive

*Lections:* Lamentations 1:1-6; Psalm 137; II Timothy 1:1-14; Luke 17:5-10

*Call to Worship*

L:  Come, let us sing of loyalty and justice:

P:  For you, O God, we will sing our songs!

L:  Come, let us tell of compassion and faith:

P:  For you, O God, we will tell our tales!

A:  A parent's love, a child's vision, a prophet's word, a sage's wisdom: For these, O God, we will proclaim your stories; for these we will praise your name!

*Invocation.* O Lord, rekindle your spirit within us; make us *burn* with your power and love. Increase our faith; set us ablaze with courage, that we might fulfill our calling before you and our neighbors—not simply because you command it, but because we demand it of ourselves.

*Litany*

L:  I see the mouths that slander the victims. Where are the ones who will honor the truth?

P:  In the name of Christ, we shall honor the truth entrusted to us by the Spirit!

L:  I see the feet that trample the captives. Where are the ones who will march for justice?

P:  In the name of Christ, we shall march for the justice entrusted to us by the Spirit!

L:  I see the hands that strike at the poor. Where are the ones who will share their abundance?

P:  In the name of Christ, we shall share the abundance entrusted to us by the Spirit!

L:  I see the backs that turn on the weak. Where are the ones who will carry with compassion?

P:  In the name of Christ, we shall carry with the compassion entrusted to us by the Spirit!

L:  I see the hearts that abandon the wayward. Where are the ones who will exercise mercy?

P:  In the name of Christ, we shall exercise the mercy entrusted to us by the Spirit!

L:  I see the eyes that despise the different. Where are the ones who will celebrate life?

P:    In the name of Christ, we shall celebrate the life entrusted
      to us by the Spirit!

*Prayer for One Voice.* O Christ, who sensed the danger of de-
pending upon others but did not hesitate to brave that danger;
who knew the pain of rebuking friends but did not hesitate to
risk that pain; who counted the cost of discipleship but did not
hesitate to pay that cost: we adore you. You are our Lord, before
whom we bow in awe and gratitude, and our Teacher, to whom
we turn in need and expectation. As you have taught us the
meaning of lordship, teach us the meaning of discipleship;
teach us what it means to be members not simply of the church
but of your body.

This is not the first time we have approached you as disciples seeking guidance. We have approached you many times,
and each time you heeded our request. But we did not always
heed your counsel. You urged us to honor those who serve God
by sharing their faith, but we coveted the honor for ourselves.
You reminded us to warn against the consequences of evil
deeds, but we feared the scorn of evildoers. You exhorted us
to treat all persons alike, in the world as in the church, but we
played favorites in the church as in the world. You have not
failed us, Lord; we have failed you.

So we come to you, asking for another chance—not a second
chance but a third or fourth or fifth chance. We ask for the grace
to hear and to heed your voice; for the fortitude to confront and
to correct our friends; for the determination to respect and to
rely on others; and for the courage to count and to pay the cost
of discipleship. We are not ignorant of the demands of discipleship, but we have not done justice by our knowledge. Help
us, O Christ, to do as well as we know and, better yet, to do the
greater works you promised we would do.

We thank you, dear Lord, for greeting us as brothers and
sisters; for making us disciples to one another, that we might
minister to one another in your spirit. Grant us the grace to be
open to one another, so that when one rejoices we all rejoice,
and when one suffers we all suffer. As the world learned of
your lordship by your love for us, let the world learn of our
discipleship by our love for one another. Rekindle within us

the gift of God; stir within us the spirit of power! Bless us, and in faith and love we will proclaim your truth.

*Benediction.* The road is long. Let us walk it with integrity of heart—seeking God and scorning evil; loving good and loathing corruption; rendering justice and righting wrong. Let us walk confidently in the power of heaven, remembering one another constantly in our prayers and honoring one another continually with our lives.[207]

## Sunday Between October 9 and October 15 Inclusive

*Lections:* Jeremiah 29:1, 4-7; Psalm 66:1-12; II Timothy 2:8-15; Luke 17:11-19

### Call to Worship

L: Make a joyful noise to God, all the earth;

P: Come and see what the Lord has done!

L: Listen, all you who suffer and wear fetters—

P: And all who are made to stand far away!

L: Lift up your voices, and cry for mercy;

P: Come before God, and be made whole again!

A: Sing with thanksgiving, and present yourselves to God! Go your way: your faith has made you well!

*Invocation.* O God, long you walked up and down upon the earth, and to and fro across the lands, but though the foxes had holes and the ravens had nests, you could find nowhere to lay your head. So we said to one another, "Let us not sleep until we make a place for the Lord, a dwelling place on earth for the Mighty One of heaven."

Thus we have prepared a room for you. Arise now, and come to us, and we will take you to ourselves, that where we are, you may be also.[208]

### Litany

L: The powers of earth may lock up the doors, but the word of the Lord will not be fettered:

---

207 Inspired by Romans 12:10.
208 Inspired by Job 1:7; Luke 9:58; Psalm 132:2-5; John 14:3; Psalm 132:8.

P: An earthquake will shake the prison's foundations, and all the chains will fall to the floor!

L: The powers of earth may blind truth's eyes, but the word of the Lord will not be weakened:

P: Its shoulders will lean on the world's pillars, and the house of sin will collapse to the ground!

L: The powers of earth may stoke their furnace, but the word of the Lord will not be consumed:

P: Its feet will walk through the midst of the fire, and even the smoke will not touch them!

L: The powers of earth may starve their lions, but the word of the Lord will not be devoured:

P: Its hand will shut the lion's mouth, and its head will sleep upon her bosom!

L: The powers of earth may erect a cross, but the word of the Lord will not die by death:

P: Its body will disappear from the grave, and its voice will haunt its enemies![209]

L: As rain showers down to water the blossoms, so is the word that comes from God's mouth:

A: It shall accomplish what the Lord has intended, and prosper in that for which it is sent![210]

*Prayer for One Voice.* O Christ of the transforming look, who sees in us what others overlook and overlooks in us what others see, we thank you for your sight, the source of our hope and the goal of our striving.

Once, upon discovering that we were blind followers of the blind, we prayed for *our* sight. But no longer. Now we pray for *your* sight, so that when we look at God, we will see not an angry judge but a gracious parent; when we look at our neighbors, we will see not objects for exploitation but partners in creation; when we look at ourselves, we will see neither a tyrant towering over others nor a servant cowering before others, but a disciple ministering unto others.

---

[209] Inspired by Acts 16:26; Judges 16:28-30; Daniel 3:19-29; 6:16-23; Acts 9:1-9.
[210] See Isaiah 55:10-11.

O Lord, as you grant us your sight, deliver us from *our* sight, which has often been a source of frustration and distortion. In our sight God has been not the dispenser of grace but the distributor of justice; our neighbors, not those to whom we could give help but those from whom we could receive help; and ourselves, not followers of your way but captives of our own. In our sight disciples have been not reformers of hearts but performers of rites. In our sight sinners have been not persons unto whom we should draw near but nobodies from whom we should steer clear. In our sight foreigners have been not a reason for celebrating the wideness of God's love but a cause for lamenting the loss of our privilege. Too long, O Lord, we have looked at the world through our own eyes, and the world has suffered the consequences of our impaired vision.

Help us, O Christ, to look at the teachings and traditions of our religion through your eyes. Should our religion claim that we believers deserve better than others, that we should be granted the friendship of the powerful and spared the company of the marginal, let us recognize that our inherited beliefs have distorted your incarnate faith. When this happens, give us the grace to acknowledge the conflict and the courage to resolve it in the spirit with which you set your face towards Jerusalem.[211] As we examine the church, endow us with the clarity of your vision, lest the gap between your church and our church grow ever wider and deeper.

We pray also, O Christ, for the gift of your sight as we examine the world. Let us behold you, enthroned in majesty at the right hand of God, staring the powers of this world in the face, refusing to render unto them what belongs to God. Let us never forget that it was for the reconciliation of the world unto God that you laid down your life. Let our eyes be anointed with your healing touch, that as we encounter the world, we might continue your work of reconciliation.

*Benediction.* The Spirit of God is impatient for faith; let us magnify our faith without boasting. The Spirit of God is impatient for hope; let us escalate our hope without hesitating. The

---

211 See Luke 9:51.

Spirit of God is impatient for peace; let us enlarge our peace without hedging. The Spirit of God is impatient for love; let us increase our love without judging.

### Sunday Between October 16 and October 22 Inclusive

*Lections:* Jeremiah 31:27-34; Psalm 119:97-104; II Timothy 3:14–4:5; Luke 18:1-8

*Call to Worship*

L: Behold, I am sending my promise upon you; believe, and be clothed with power from on high!

P: Your spirit is rushing upon us with power; your wind is filling this house with heaven!

L: My promise is sent to you and your children—to all who stand far away from me![212]

P: Your tongues of fire rest upon all flesh! Make us see visions, and let us dream dreams; help us take heart, and prophesy![213]

*Invocation.* O God, your promise of faithfulness is well tried; we have tested it time and again. Though sometimes we have delighted in it, we have often distrusted it, defied it, deserted it. But our lack of faith could never destroy it.

O Lord, we are foolish; grant us understanding, according to your promise, and we will live your life. We are timid; grant us courage, and we will do your work. We are broken; grant us healing, and we will love your word.

*Litany*

L: The Lord set me down in the midst of a valley filled with old, dry bones. And as commanded, I prophesied, and declared to the bones a living word.

P: And behold, a mighty rattling was heard as the bones were knitted together; then flesh came upon them, and life breathed in their souls, and they leaped to their feet to dance a great dance.[214]

---

212 See Luke 24:49; Acts 1:8; 2:2, 39.
213 Inspired by Acts 2:3, 17-18.
214 See Ezekiel 37:1-10.

A: The vision awaits its time of fulfillment; let us be patient, but never be idle!

L: The Lord touched my mouth with a burning coal, and told me to speak to the people.[215] And as commanded, I prophesied, and declared to the nations a living word.

P: You told of the wolf that dwelled with the lamb, of the calf and the lion that walked together with a little child before them; of the child who played over the hole of the serpent, while all earth lived in the knowledge of God.[216]

A: The vision awaits its time of fulfillment; let us be patient, but never be idle!

L: I heard behind me a voice like a trumpet, saying, "Write what you see in a book." And as commanded, I prophesied, and declared to the world a living word.

P: You wrote of a heaven and an earth made new, of former things passed away; of a holy city come down from God, who promised to make a home on earth, who wiped the tears from our eyes and caused our mourning to be no more![217]

A: The vision awaits its time of fulfillment; let us be patient, but never be idle! The Messiah is coming; let faith be found!

*Prayer for One Voice.* O God of compassionate prophets, hear us now, though we have been neither compassionate nor prophetic. We have witnessed the workings of your word through the Moseses and the Miriams, through the Daniels and the Deborahs—through those who lived long before us and through those who live among us. You have caused their eyes to see wrongs and to look upon troubles. Their souls have watched until your fire was kindled within them, and they began to rage against the destruction and violence being wrought, at the contention and strife being waged. Your prophets see, and seethe, and finally speak—but do we hear? Have we faith?

How fearful we are, Lord, of our world as it is; but how much more fearful of what it might take to make it different! When

---

215 Inspired by Isaiah 6:6, 9.

216 See Isaiah 11:6-9.

217 See Revelation 1:10; 21:1-5.

your prophets counsel peace, we are afraid to lay down our arms. So we remind the prophets that Christ said, "You have heard that you shall love your neighbor and hate your enemy," forgetting that in the next moment, he declared, "I say love your enemies and pray for those who persecute you." When your prophets denounce poverty, we are afraid to give up our wealth. So we remind the prophets that Christ said, "You will always have the poor with you," forgetting that in the next breath, he declared, "Do good to them." When your prophets decry prejudice, we are afraid to share our status. So we remind the prophets that Christ said, "I was sent only to the house of Israel; I will not throw the children's bread to the dogs," forgetting that in the next moment, he declared, "O Canaanite woman, great is your faith! Be it done as you desire!" When your prophets attack false piety, we are afraid to confess our pride. So we remind the prophets that Christ said, "This people honors me with their lips," forgetting that in the next breath, he declared, "But their heart is far from me; they leave the commandment of God and hold fast to their own traditions."[218]

Again and again, O God, you have raised up your prophets; again and again you have made their lips burn—but we have been more willing to rid ourselves of them than to risk ourselves for you. So if you would change our world, you will need to change *us!* Send your spirit upon *us;* make *our* souls burn; make *us* your messengers, that we might declare an end to the destruction and violence and contention and strife of which we once were the agents.

Change us, Lord; make us your people: a people equipped not merely for work, but for *good* work; a people prepared not merely for life, but for *faithful* life; a people united not merely in spirit, but in a *gracious* spirit; a people inspired not merely by love, but by an *inexhaustible, unquenchable* love. Change us, and in your name we shall curse enmity, and war shall be no more; we shall curse poverty, and want shall be no more; we shall curse prejudice, and bigotry shall be no more; we shall curse false piety, and hypocrisy shall be no more. Change us; make us whole, and when your

218 See Matthew 5:43-44; Mark 14:7; Matthew 15:26-28; Mark 7:6-7.

word is spoken, when Christ is come among us, there will, indeed, be found a people of faith on earth.

*Benediction*

L: Let us lead a life worthy of our calling;

P: Let us fulfill our ministry in the Lord;

L: With humility and patience, forbearing in love,

P: Let us maintain our unity in the bond of peace—[219]

A: Until all achieve maturity of faith and attain to the stature of Christ![220]

## *Sunday Between October 23 and October 29 Inclusive*

*Lections:* Joel 2:23-32; Psalm 65; II Timothy 4:6-8, 16-18; Luke 18:9-14

*Call to Worship*

L: O sinners, let us cleanse our hearts!

P: O people, let us purify our minds!

L: Come, let us submit ourselves to the Lord,

P: And humble ourselves before our God![221]

L: Let us pray and sing and seek God's face, and turn from our selfish ways,

P: That God might hear and forgive our sin, and heal our wounded world![222]

*Invocation.* We cry to you, O God; answer us! Be merciful to us who have sinned! Rescue us from the lion's mouth! We have been cast into the den, a stone has sealed us in—we cannot save ourselves.[223] We are not Daniel—our faith is frail—but stand by us and give us strength, and we will prevail. We will boldly proclaim your word, through the witness of our lips and the works of our lives!

---

219 See Ephesians 4:1; Colossians 4:17; Ephesians 4:2, 3.

220 Inspired by Ephesians 4:13.

221 See James 4:7-10.

222 Inspired by II Chronicles 7:14-15.

223 Inspired by Daniel 6:16-23.

*Litany*

L: Blessed is the land whose people trust not in themselves but in the Lord:

P: Whose leaders proclaim not their awesome deeds but the mighty acts of God;

L: Whose ministers, when they pray, do not say, "God, I thank you that I am not like other people";

P: Whose citizens beat upon their breasts and say, "God, be merciful to me, a sinner!"

L: Whose judges are upright in all their deeds, and just in all their ways;

P: Whose public servants hear the cry of the oppressed, and fulfill the desires of the needy;

L: Whose laborers not only praise the divine name, but imitate the divine character;

P: Whose elders dream dreams, and look not to yesterday but to tomorrow;

L: Whose youths see visions, and strive to put flesh on them;

P: Whose prophets not only fight the good fight and finish the race, but keep the faith—

A: That all might call on the name of the Lord, and praise God from one generation to another!

*Prayer for One Voice.* O Christ our Lord, support of the righteous and troubler of the self-righteous, help of the faithful and hope of the faithless, you are our refuge and strength, a very present help in trouble. Not only are you there just *when* we need you most. You are there just *as* we need you most: to confront us when we need to be confronted; to comfort us when we need to be comforted; to correct us when we need to be corrected; to commend us when we need to be commended. You are the answer—not only to our prayer but to our need. So we thank you for your readiness to honor us with your presence and for your determination to transform us *by* your presence.

From the dawn of history until the present, you have been with us, leading us away from temptation into the paths of righteousness. You endowed us with all the gifts necessary to discern your presence among us. You gave us a heart for understanding your motives, a mind for deciphering your will, eyes for discovering your purpose, ears for hearing your summons, and hands and feet for performing your commands. Yet we have let these gifts lie dormant. And now we and our world are in trouble—not because of your absence but because of our insensitivity to your presence.

You have been present to instruct us in the ways of peace with justice. You tried to teach us the wisdom of turning swords into plowshares, but we have turned them into tanks and missiles. You tried to teach us the wisdom of preventing conflict by eliminating hunger, but we have played politics and ignored poverty. You tried to teach us the wisdom of using persuasion rather than coercion, but we have practiced intimidation. With shame we confess, O Lord, that we could have learned a great deal more from our history, if only we had acknowledged your presence and heeded your instruction. We must also confess that we have not profited as we should from your presence in the lives of your faithful ones. In them you gave us clues to your will, but we have preferred to follow our own.

Forgive us, O Christ, for having been such inept students of history and of humanity. Enable us to learn from experience—our own as well as the experience of others; help us to profit from mistakes—the mistakes of others as well as our own. Let us feel your presence at work in others for our sake; let others feel your presence at work in us for their sake.

*Benediction.* The time of our departure has come. Stand by us, O God, and give us strength, that we might fight the good fight, and run the good race, and keep the faith, from this day forth and forever.

## *Sunday Between October 30 and November 5 Inclusive*

*Lections:* Habakkuk 1:1-4; 2:1-4; Psalm 119:137-144; II Thessalonians 1:1-4, 11-12; Luke 19:1-10

*Call to Worship*
L: Strife and contention are before us;
P: Destruction and violence are on every side.
L: But the law of the Lord is true,
P: And the righteousness of the Lord is forever.

A: Brothers, raise your Hallelujah! Sisters, sing Hosanna! This glorious day belongs to the Lord: This world of woe shall be transformed!

*Invocation.* O God of our salvation, you are our hope! Yesterday your wisdom established the mountains; today your power stills the seas; tomorrow your peace will unite the peoples. This is our conviction—and this, our calling: that we should bear your wisdom and power and peace in a world stumbling in its folly, fainting in its weakness, succumbing to its violence. Endow us, O Lord, with the courage to walk in your way, the strength to stand for your cause, and the compassion to live out your will—not that *we* might be saved, but that, through us, you might save the world.

*Litany*

L: Zacchaeus climbed a sycamore tree—he couldn't see over the people;

P: Who else will rise above the crowd to see salvation come?

L: Zacchaeus climbed a sycamore tree, then hurried down when Christ called him;

P: Who else will ignore the scorn of foes to answer a righteous Lord?

L: Zacchaeus climbed a sycamore tree, then gave away his goods;

P: Who else will dare to confess their sin and try to make fourfold amends?

L: Zacchaeus climbed a sycamore tree, then spread at his house a sinners' feast;

P: Who else will prepare a table for Christ and for every soul the town despises?

L: Who else will look on Christ and grow? Who else will admit they're not yet grown?

P: Who else will climb to glimpse the Lord when the road is blocked from view? Who else will open the door to the poor because, once lost, they now are found?

*Prayer for One Voice.* O Spirit, you are the voice that will never fail to sing, though all the world be silent; you are the foot that will never fail to dance, though all the world be still. You are

171

the eye that will never fail to watch, though all the world be sleeping; you are the mind that will never fail to reason, though all the world be senseless. You are the hand that will never fail to open, though all the world be selfish; you are the heart that will never fail to feel, though all the world be numb.

Thank you, Spirit, for abiding in our midst, for moving us when we do not want to move and for slowing us down when we do not want to stop. Thank you for moving in ways that, though mysterious, do not frighten us away. We are a people often made small by the greatness of our fear. We shrink from conflict when conflict cries out for resolution. We flee from truth when truth demands expression. We run from change when change must come: change that will require us to be no longer who we have been, to do no longer as we have done, to say no longer what we have said, to believe no longer as we have believed.

O Comforter, remain among us, and we will rise above our fear. Instead of shrinking from conflict, we will join it until it is justly resolved. Instead of fleeing from truth, we will pursue it until it is freely expressed. Instead of running from change, we will weigh it until it is fairly judged.

O Spirit, abide among us, and we will rise above all fear. We will become your voice, and though all else be silent, we will never cease to sing your song. We will become your feet, and though all else be still, we will never cease to dance your dance. We will become your eyes, and though all else be sleeping, we will never cease to keep your watch. We will become your mind, and though all else be senseless, we will never cease to seek your will. We will become your hands, and though all else be selfish, we will never cease to share your riches. We will become your heart, and though all else be numb, we will never fail to love your world.

*Benediction.* Let us take heart and labor diligently for the reign of God. May the grace of God complete every good work through the power of faith, that we might praise God with our lips and glorify Christ with our lives.

SEASON AFTER PENTECOST

## Sunday Between November 6 and November 12 Inclusive

*Lections:* Haggai 1:15b–2:9; Psalm 145:1-5, 17-21; II Thessalonians 2:1-5, 13-17; Luke 20:27-38

*Call to Worship*

L: Come, let us sing together, and our hymns shall ascend to the sun, the heart of God—

P: The Lord our God, who is worthy of praise!

L: Come, let us dance together, and our rhythms shall shake the earth, the footstool of God—[224]

P: The Lord our God, who is worthy of trust!

A: Let us sing and dance; let us clap and shout! Our God is the God of the living, and we have been reborn!

*Invocation.* O God, be mindful of your covenant with us, and we will be mindful of the wonders you work among us[225]—the wonder of your forgiveness, being anxious to reconcile; the wonder of your patience, being slow to anger; the wonder of your mercy, being abundant in love; the wonder of your faithfulness, being loathe to forsake. Arise, O God; make yourself known, and all will be changed into your likeness as we behold your glory.[226]

*Litany*

L: When the tomb looms large before our eyes, remind us, Lord, of who we are:

P: We are children of the resurrection; the place of death will not hold us.

L: We are the painters of the rainbows; the shadow of death will not daunt us.

P: We are the breakers of loaves and fishes; the taste of death will not defile us.

L: We are the equals of the angels; the threat of death will not deter us.

P: We are the raisers of the dead; the power of death will not defy us.

---

224 Inspired by Isaiah 66:1.

225 Inspired by I Chronicles 16:15.

226 See II Corinthians 3:18.

L:  We are the fanners of the flames; the wind of death will not defeat us.

P:  We are the people of Pentecost; the spirit of death will not destroy us![227]

*Prayer for One Voice.* O God of parables and riddles, how you tantalize our minds by your glory! We marvel at your universe, stretching beyond the reach of any human eye or telescope; we behold infinity in a blade of grass and eternity in a drop of water. The vision of life is too great—it blinds us; we raise our hands, we turn our heads from the brilliant light. Relieve the burning magnificence of your presence, Lord; do you not know that we are only human?

O God of mysteries and secrets, how you tempt us by your love! We wonder at your faithfulness, stretching beyond the reach of any human heart or promise; we feel boundless compassion at the touch of your hand and endless forgiveness at the sound of your voice. The experience of your love is too much—it dazes us; we fall on our knees, we reach for you in the trembling air. Relieve the overwhelming fullness of your presence, Lord; do you not know that we are only human?

O, but you do know! You have endured long centuries of our sinful ways, and your ears have grown heavy from our monotonous defense: "We are only human, Lord!" we have said; "You expect too much!" Your heart has groaned as we have wrestled with your angels, crying, "How can we mortals be righteous before God? How can we human beings be pure before our Maker? How can the Lord trust us, who dwell in houses of clay, who are crushed before the moth? How can the Holy One have faith in us, who drink iniquity like water?"[228] Your heart has broken as we have contended with your heavens, shouting, "*You do not need us!* How can a human be profitable to a god? Surely in your power you require no help!"[229]

Yes, Lord; you know well that we are only mortal, for only we have been so proud as to declare our utter independence

---

227 Inspired by Genesis 9; Matthew 14:15-21; John 11:38-44; Hebrews 1:7; Acts 2:1-4.

228 See Job 4:17-20; 15:16.

229 Inspired by Job 22:2.

from you in one breath and our utter dependence upon you in the next. And only we, among all your creatures, have dared to question your goodness in creating us and our dignity in *being* us; we have equated our existence with that of the miserable worm,[230] as if you had not also made the worm and provided for its place!

O God, remind us that being "only human" is not meant to be a cause for shame, but celebration. We are yours—your children, your people; and like our sister, the caterpillar,[231] we are born to be reborn, to awaken from sleep to the spirit, and to put on the colorful clothes of your glory and love.

Convince us, Lord, of the truth of your parables and riddles; persuade us of the revelation of your mysteries and secrets. For all that is revealed is One: All that is revealed is You, who are the union of Life and Love. Let us stop degrading our humanity by appealing to our weakness. We are children of deity, humanity born of heaven. To abase ourselves is to blaspheme you. To separate ourselves from you is to commit sacrilege against you. Let the words of our lips increase the word of your mouth; let the works of our lives magnify the work of your hand!

*Benediction.* Let us live to God, remembering that we are children of the resurrection and equals of the angels. Let us render true judgments, showing kindness and mercy, that the saving word of the Lord might triumph over all malice and every cruelty, in this world as in the next.

## Sunday Between November 13 and November 19 Inclusive

*Lections:* Isaiah 65:17-25; Isaiah 12; II Thessalonians 3:6-13; Luke 21:5-19

*Call to Worship*
L:  I am about to create new heavens and a new earth—
P:  No more shall be heard the cry of grief or distress!
L:  The sun of justice will set no more;[232]

---

230 See Psalm 22:6.
231 Inspired by Job 17:14.
232 Inspired by Isaiah 60:19-20.

P: It circles the heavens above us, borne by winds of blessing!
L: The light will shine forever;
P: It shall not be overcome![233]
L: Its rays are descending—let them embrace you;
P: Let us become radiant,[234] and learn to fly!

*Invocation.* O Lord, the earth is reeling, the foundations of the mountains tremble and quake;[235] we stumble in shadows over the shaking ground, looking neither left nor right. We are blind to the great light,[236] and we are blind to those on whom the light has shone—the weak and the forsaken, the afflicted and the tormented, the powerless and the poor.

Restore our sight, Lord. Lead us out of the shadows of indifference into the glory of faithfulness, that one day the world might reel from rejoicing; that one day the foundations of the earth might tremble beneath the pounding of dancing feet.

*Litany*
L: The day of the Lord our God has come—
P: It burns like a fiery oven!
L: Wickedness bursts into flame and is gone;
P: Its ashes cover the ground at our feet.
L: Fire will test the work we have done—
P: This is no coal for warming oneself,
L: This is no home-fire to rest beside!
P: Yet the Lord has told us not to fear
L: When we walk through the fire we shall not be burned;
P: The flames shall not consume us.[237]
L: Like the bush that caused Moses to turn aside,[238]
P: We shall blaze with the dazzling glory of God,
L: Being refined in its heat like silver and gold,
P: Reliving our baptism of Pentecost fire![239]

---

233 See John 1:5.
234 Inspired by Matthew 13:43.
235 See Psalm 18:7.
236 Inspired by Isaiah 9:2.
237 See I Corinthians 3:13; Isaiah 47:14; 43:1-2.
238 Inspired by Exodus 3:3.
239 See Malachi 3:2-3; Acts 2:3.

L:  O Spirit, ignite the world with your lightning—
P:  You are the spark; make us your fuel!

*Prayer for One Voice.* O God of heaven and earth, your prophets and apostles teach us to anticipate "the day of the Lord"—a time when wrong will be righted and the righteous honored, when violence will be rejected and the peacemakers acclaimed, when injustice will be outlawed and the just praised, when guilt will be acknowledged and the innocent acquitted. We give thanks that you are our God, for only a God like you can breathe hope into our life and grant meaning to our existence.

Enable us, O Lord, when we think of your day, to remember the character of the One whose day it is. Help us to put the emphasis where it belongs: not on the fact you *will be* our Judge but on the fact you *are* our Judge; not on your power to wound us then but on our power to wound you now. Let us not forget that the Lord whom we shall meet on your day is no other than the One we have met in Jesus Christ our Lord, in whom you have warned us of the evils you deplore and alerted us to the virtues you uphold.

O God, you warn us not to think more highly of ourselves than we ought, but we honor ourselves before our neighbors. You warn us not to return evil for evil, but we seek an eye for an eye. You warn us that your gospel can turn friends into enemies, but we are anxious if all do not speak well of us. Yes, Lord, you warn us of the evils you deplore, but we do not shun them. Sadder but wiser, we pray for another chance.

We also fail to embrace the virtues to which you alert us. You appeal to us to grant justice to the weak, but we continue to concede privilege to the strong. You appeal to us to show partiality to the orphan, but we question our responsibility to atone for inequity. You appeal to us to maintain the rights of the afflicted, but we regard their defense as a charity case. You appeal to us to rescue the needy, but we stand idly by while their numbers multiply. Yes, Lord, you call us to the virtues you uphold, but we do not embrace them. Sadder but wiser, we pray for another chance.

Forgive us, O God, for our insensitivity to your warnings and appeals and, even more, to the agony of those in whose behalf you utter them. Bestow on us the gifts of your Holy Spirit, that we might become agents of your will, taking your warnings to heart and heeding your appeals. As we go forth in your name, grant us the faith that moves people, the hope that builds community, and the love that creates family.

*Benediction.* May God give you wisdom that no adversary will be able to refute. May God give you power that no adversary will be able to resist. And may God give you compassion, that no adversary will be able to refuse.

## Christ the King

*Lections:* Jeremiah 23:1-6; Luke 1:68-79; Colossians 1:11-20; Luke 23:33-43

*Call to Worship*
L:  In the image of Christ we are created;
P:  In the spirit of Christ we are knit together.
L:  In the body of Christ we are reborn;
P:  In the love of Christ we are reconciled.
L:  O come, let us sing Hosanna to God—
P:  Whose fullness in Christ was pleased to dwell,
A:  Whose fullness in us desires to live!

*Invocation.* O Christ, the time for celebration has arrived! Come among us, and we will run to meet you with cries of "Savior!" We will greet you as our messiah—not because you have wrought many miracles, but because you execute justice and righteousness. Our adulation will cause your enemies to reach out their hands, saying, "Remember us when you come into your kingdom!"

   O Messiah, come among us! Come among us in the name of the Lord!

*Litany*
L:  The Lord our God is a great God—
P:  A God above all gods, Lord of all lands and peoples!
L:  The depths of the earth rest in God's hand;
P:  The crests of the mountains gaze over God's palm.

L:  The mighty waters obey God's voice—
P:  The voice that commanded them to appear.
L:  The dry lands know the touch of God's fingers—
P:  The fingers that formed them to bring forth life.
L:  Thus, from their dust we have been born:[240]
P:  Woman and man, in the image of God.[241]
L:  Why do we then let our hearts be hardened?
P:  Why do we put our Maker to the test?
L:  Why do we doubt our very bones?
P:  Why do we scorn our Creator's ways?
L:  The Lord our God is a God above gods;
A:  Let us worship the Lord with songs of praise!

*Prayer for One Voice.* O Maker of covenants and Keeper of promises, you are the cornerstone of our faith and the foundation of our hope!

You are the Rock, opening yourself so that water might flow for those wandering in the wilderness;

You are the Rock, raising yourself up amid desert wastes to offer shade in a weary land;

You are the Rock, making yourself level when the way is rough, that the foot of the traveler might be secure;

You are the Rock, speaking when no other voice is heard and hearing when no other ear is bent;[242]

You are the Rock, in which there is no unrighteousness, in which there is great refuge;[243]

You are the Rock, from which the death-tomb is hewn, and you are the stone, rolling away from its door;

You are the Rock, from which your people are fashioned, and on which our house and your kingdom stand![244]

Yes, Lord, you are our Rock: the cornerstone of our faith and the foundation of our hope. Therefore, we pray, strengthen us with all power, according to your glorious might, that we may

---

240 Inspired by Genesis 1:10, 11-12; 2:7.

241 See Genesis 1:27.

242 Inspired by Psalm 95:1; Exodus 17:6-7; Isaiah 32:2; Psalm 40:2; II Samuel 23:3; Psalm 28:1.

243 See Psalm 92:15; II Samuel 22:2.

244 Inspired by Luke 23:53; 24:2; Isaiah 51:1; Matthew 7:24; 16:8.

be filled with the endurance of your mountains, standing against rain and wind and earthquake and fire. Strengthen us, that we may be filled with the patience of your rivers, flowing against forces intent on slowing them down or damming them up. Strengthen us, that we may be filled with the joy of your harvest, singing as the fields are crowned with bounty and the valleys are clothed with grain.[245]

O God, as in Christ all your fullness was pleased to dwell, so make us fit vessels for your indwelling spirit. As through Christ you sought to reconcile all things, so make us instruments of your reconciliation. And as by Christ you worked to establish peace, so make us agents of your peacemaking.

You are our salvation, Lord. Standing on any other ground, we can do nothing; standing on you, we can do everything.[246] Sinking in sand, all is impossible; building on rock, all things are possible.[247] In the name of all that can be done, in the spirit of all that is possible, we commit ourselves to your cause, our Strength and our Redeemer!

*Benediction.* May the love of Christ strengthen you with all power. May you endure with all hope and persevere with all joy, until all things in heaven and on earth are reconciled in a just and lasting peace.

---

245 See Psalm 65:11-13.
246 See Philippians 4:13.
247 Inspired by Matthew 19:26; 7:24-27.

# Celebration of Special Occasions

## New Year's Eve/Day

*Lections:* Ecclesiastes 3:1-13; Psalm 8; Revelation 21:1-6a; Matthew 25:31-46

*Call to Worship*
L: We gather to bid farewell to the old year, a year that brought burdens and blessings.
P: We thank you, O God, for the strength to bear its burdens and the grace to share its blessings.
L: We gather to bid welcome to the new year, a year that harbors perils and promises.
P: We ask you, O God, for the courage to master its perils and the wisdom to realize its promises.
L: The Lord joins us to redeem our memories of the year past and to rekindle our hopes for the year ahead. Let us rejoice and be glad!

*Invocation.* O God, who changes old years into new years that we might explore your purpose for life, guide us in our search. Let us so behold the world through your eyes that, instead of turning back to our past, we can look ahead to your future; that, instead of trying to fit you into our plans for changing the world, you can fit us into *your* plans for changing the world; that, instead of this year being simply a repeat of last year, it can be a truly *new* year—a year in which you light up our life and we light up your world.

*Litany*
L: The New Year is a time for taking stock of our life.
P: O Lord, you know us better than we know ourselves. Help us to look at ourselves through your eyes.
L: Let us reflect on our use of time,
P: And resolve to deepen our experience of eternity.
L: Let us reflect on our investment of money,
P: And resolve to live our understanding of stewardship.

181

L: Let us reflect on our attitude toward work,
P: And resolve to strengthen our sense of vocation.
L: Let us reflect on our regard for leisure,
P: And resolve to respect our need for renewal.
L: Let us reflect on our perception of friendship,
P: And resolve to broaden our definition of family.
L: The New Year is a time for letting go and taking hold.
P: O Lord, you know us better than we know ourselves.
   Help us to let go of the things that pass away, that we
   might take hold of the things that endure.

*Prayer for One Voice.* O God, our help in years gone by and our
hope for years to come, we bow before you in awe and wonder.
When we consider the gifts with which you blessed our yesterdays and the marvels with which you will bless our tomorrows, we are left speechless. In vain we search for words to
express our gratitude. You are not only a great and powerful
God. You are a good and gracious God—a God anxious to keep
covenant with those who heed your summons; a God even
more anxious to *make* covenant with those who do not.

We have heard and heeded your summons to join the
covenantal community. Yet we resist your call to widen its
circle. We are more concerned with retaining its privileges for
ourselves than with sharing its benefits with others. Instead of
following the one who spurned equality with you to become
the servant of all, we spurn the role of servant to seek equality
with you. Though we say that Christ is making all things new,
few people see evidence of his transforming power in us. They
hear us claim to be Christ's servants, but they are struck by our
neglect of those whom Jesus served. They hear us boast of
being one body, but they are amazed by the strife among our
members. So they turn away from Christ because we turn them
away from Christ.

O God, we ask your forgiveness. We are honestly sorry for
misrepresenting you, for deceiving others, and for betraying
ourselves. Grant us the grace to greet this New Year as new
people. Give us a new vision of your mission and the will to
make it our own. Give us a new recognition of your hatred of
falsehood, and the courage to enlist in the struggle for truth.

Give us a new zeal for the pursuit of peace with justice, and the determination to achieve it in our lifetime. Give us a new understanding of your long-hidden plan, and the readiness to live by it on earth as in heaven.

O Lord, you have invited us to sit at a table from which none is excluded. You have promised abundant life to all who hear and heed your call. Now is the time, dear Lord. Break bread with us! Renew your promise! As we welcome the dawn of another New Year, send us forth to herald your summons. Send us into the streets and lanes, into the highways and byways, that all the world might partake of the promise in Christ Jesus through the gospel.

*Benediction.* O God, as we enter the new year, help us to abandon the pursuit of treasures which moth and rust corrupt and thieves break in and steal. Set us on a journey toward a faith that success cannot adorn or failure dim; toward a hope that ambition cannot hasten or frustration delay; toward a love that praise cannot cheapen or scorn subdue.

## *Epiphany*

*Lections:* Isaiah 60:1-6; Psalm 72:1-14; Ephesians 3:1-12; Matthew 2:1-12

*Call to Worship*
L: O come, let us worship the Lord, and consider what wondrous things God has done:
P: The magi who study the heavens follow a guiding star!
L: O come, let us worship the Lord, and consider what wondrous things God has done:
P: The exiles who dwell in the shadows see a glorious light!
L: O come, let us worship the Lord, and consider what wondrous things God has done:
P: The Christ who embodies the word unveils the hidden plan,
L: Making all people joint heirs of the promise of salvation through the gospel!
A: O come, let us worship the Lord, for God *has* done wondrous things!

*Invocation.* O God, who quickens the faith that brings magi from the East, who kindles the hope that brings captives from exile, and who inspires the love that brings strangers together, let the light that shone in the darkness shine upon us. Let it shine within us, that it might consume the dross that corrupts our hearts. Let it shine *around* us, that it might illumine the way that leads to our neighbors. And let it shine *above* us, that it might reveal the Christ who manifests your presence.

## Litany

L:  God commanded the light of divine glory to shine out of the darkness,[248]

P:  And we beheld that light in the face of Jesus Christ our Lord.

L:  We stood and gazed, as if given an idol on which to muse,

P:  But we quickly learned that it was a lamp by which to see the truth.

L:  Its light reveals God's heavenly will for all earthly rulers,

P.  That they might establish justice and righteousness throughout the earth;

L:  That they might be like the gentle rains that fall upon the grass,[249]

P:  Renewing the hope of the hungry for food and the stricken for relief;

L:  That they might be like belated showers that drench a thirsty land,

P:  Restoring the strength of the weak and the faith of the despondent;

L:  That they might be like the sun by day and the moon and stars by night,

P:  Reviving the joy of the sorrowful and the fellowship of the forsaken.

A:  Rejoice and make merry! The light that was shining there and then is shining here and now!

---

248 Inspired by II Corinthians 4:6.
249 See Isaiah 9:7; Psalm 72:6.

*Prayer for One Voice.* O Lord, our God, who can abide no rule that is not righteous and no judgment that is not just, we adore you.

You are far from us in being, and even farther from us in goodness—so far that we could never hope to bridge the gap from our side to yours. Yet you, O Lord, could and did bridge the gap from your side to ours. Though not a human being, you appeared among us as a human being. Though not of this world, you joined us in this world. In Christ you ended the separation between Creator and creature; in Christ you broke down the wall between yourself and your world. In Christ you revealed your glory and reconciled us unto yourself, and for this we praise your name.

Yet we do not come to you as, in Christ, you came to us. We hail Jesus Christ as the light of the world, but we resist the summons to become his light in the world.[250] We call ourselves his disciples, but we are slow to embrace his mission. We pray for his reign to come on earth, but we shun the people he came to rule. As Jesus taught, we give food to the hungry; we give water to the thirsty; we give clothing to the naked; we give medicine to the sick—but unlike Christ, we do not give *ourselves*.

Forgive us, O God, for proclaiming your incarnation in Christ, yet living as if Christ need not become incarnate in us; for hailing his teaching, yet failing to follow his example; and for reducing his revelation of your love into just another revelation of the law. Let the light that led the shepherds and the magi lead us into the secret places of the Most High. And let the light shine within us until it turns our hearts, as it turned theirs, upward to you in worship, and outward to the world in service.

When Jesus Christ appeared on earth, heaven and nature joined the mighty chorus that sang your praise and his. Sages from the East were guided by a star to the place where he lay. We are still guided—or perhaps misguided—by stars in our search for his presence. Perhaps we ought to be following not the path of stars, but of hurricanes and earthquakes and tor-

---

250 Inspired by Philippians 2:15.

nados—of catastrophes that shred nature's beauty with the first blow and decimate our security with the second. Multitudes have become victims of such calamities. If we have not yet found our way to these victims, help us, dear Lord, to follow the One who has. Help us to find Christ in the world, that we might become Christ to the world.

Even though much misery stems from natural calamity, we must confess that much stems from human action or, just as often, human inaction. We not only *know* its source; we *are* its source. Misery springs from us: from our heads, our hands, our hearts. We do not consider the needs of the needy until they join the ranks of the wretched. We do not face the fact of their insecurity until they threaten our security; neither do we discover the denial of their humanity until they begin to rob us of our humanity.

O light of the world, illumine us—our minds, that they might think the thoughts of Christ; our hearts, that they might feel the compassion of Christ; our hands, that they might do the deeds of Christ—that through our lives you might illumine the world.

*Benediction.* O God, whose holy light quenched the fear of the shepherds and the timidity of the magi, illumine our lives as you illumined theirs. Let the light that flooded Bethlehem's manger so transform us that, when temptation comes, we shall neither go astray nor lead astray; when calamity strikes, we shall neither grope blindly nor stagger feebly; and when the summons comes, we shall neither forget you nor forsake our neighbor.

## Human Relations Day/Martin Luther King, Jr., Day

*Lections:* Micah 4:1-5; Psalm 37:1-6, 23-28, 39-40; Colossians 3:12-17; Matthew 5:43-48

*Call to Worship*
L:  Come, let us join our souls, and we shall pray to the Lord for hope—
P:  For many are the dreams that die, strangled by the hands of despair.

L: Come, let us join our spirits, and we shall pray to the
   Lord for compassion—
P: For many are the backs that bleed, beaten by the whip of
   rage.
L: Come, let us join our wills, and we shall pray to the Lord
   for peace—
P: For many are the wounds that fester, inflicted by the
   sword of strife.
L: Come, let us join our hearts, and we shall pray to the Lord
   for love—
P: For many are the ties that break, severed by the knife of
   hate.
A: Make us one, O Lord, that many might be the ties that
   bind, the wounds that mend, the backs that heal, and
   the dreams that come to pass!

*Invocation.* O Justice, whose word is the sound of the chain
being broken and the sight of the captive being released, receive our prayer! The chains of our world clank and rattle; the
captives groan and cry! Homes and homelands, near and far,
are peopled by broken hearts, battered bodies, wasted minds,
shattered lives. Principalities and powers steal dignity and
inflict poverty, deceive trust and breed suspicion, destroy the
will and foster indifference.

O Lord, whether we be captor or captive, let your word come
among us. Let it dwell within us, that we might burst every
chain asunder and cause the captive to cry out for joy!

*Litany*
L: Let us not seek our own welfare and neglect the care of
   another,
P: Lest we fade like the grass and wither like the weed;
L: For the sun of God shines upon the cruel, as upon the
   kind—
P: If our roots do not run down into good soil, the sun shall
   cause our flower to wilt; its rays shall make our leaves
   to shrivel.
L: Let us not pursue our own desires by inflicting pain on another,

187

P: Lest we drown like the seed and wash away like the stalk;

L: For the rain of God descends upon the cruel, as upon the kind—

P: If our roots do not reach deep into firm ground, the rain shall choke our fragile shoot; its torrents shall wrest us from the earth.

L: No, let us commit our life to the Lord,

P: That *all* might flourish beneath the sun and be nourished by the rain.

L: Let the hand of the Lord increase the fruits of our labor, that the harvest might yield plenty—not for one but for all;

P: Let the hand of the Lord pluck the barbs from our branches and cast them into the fire,

A: Lest they be gleaned by calloused hands and woven into a crown of thorns.

*Prayer for One Voice.* O Giver of hope, who inspires dreams and brings them to fulfillment, we turn to you with tender hearts. Some of our hearts are tender because they are compassionate; others, because they are in pain—in pain that so many dreams should have been born only to die cruel deaths. Or so it seems. The dream that all people, whatever the color of their skin, would see that they are created equal—like a star that flashes across the sky, this dream seems to have faded. The dream that all people, whatever the land of their home, would lay down their arms and learn war no more—like the grape that shrivels on the vine, this dream seems to have perished. The dream that all people, whatever the language of their faith, would behold the realm of heaven on earth—like a lover who leaves for a moment and never returns, this dream seems to have passed away.

O God, we are the ones you anoint to keep dreams alive and, if they are dead, to resurrect them! We are the ones you lead to the mountaintop, there to give us visions of the Promised Land! But when you send us back down into the valley, down into the crowded ways of life, we become afraid. The gap between your revelation and our reality seems too great for any bridge. So we stop our ears against the sound of your voice, and resolve

188

never again to return to the mountaintop. Dreams are abandoned; revelations, scorned; expectations, lowered.

This we confess, Lord: We are terrified by dreams that are not our own. We cannot fulfill them through *our* strength; we have lent our strength to our own dreams. We cannot fulfill them through our hope; we have lent our hope to our own ambitions. We cannot fulfill them through our faith; we have lent our faith to our own idols.

Change us, O Lord, that the world might change! Turn to us with a tender heart—tender, because compassionate; tender, because in pain—in pain that you should have placed so many dreams in our hands, only to have us twist them into nightmares. Call us again to the mountaintop, with a voice so compelling it cannot be ignored. Blind us again with *your* vision of the Promised Land, and heal our sight, that we might see it clearly. Bring us to the day when all your dreams become ours, when all your dreams will come true—when all people, whatever the color of their skin, see that they are created equal; when all people, whatever the land of their home, learn war no more; when all people, whatever the language of their faith, behold the realm of heaven on earth.

Bring us to the day when the falling star will be fixed in the sky forever; when the ripening grape will be pressed into the everlasting wine of communion; when the immortal lover shall return to lie down in the bosom of the earth, and, sleeping, live again.

*Benediction.* The day will come when the mountain of the Lord shall tower above every mountain, and all the earth's peoples shall camp at its feet. On that day the word of the Lord shall roll down like thunder, and the glory of the Lord shall be revealed. Every valley shall be exalted, and every hill brought low; the rough places shall be made smooth, and the crooked places, straight. Justice shall cover the earth as waters cover the sea, and we shall overcome!

# LITANIES AND OTHER PRAYERS

## *Festival of the Home/Intergenerational Celebration*

*Lections:* Isaiah 51:1-8; Psalm 112; III John 1-6, 11-15; Matthew 6:25-33

### *Call to Worship*

L:   We gather as members of the family of God,

P:   Who long to be happy in the Lord and with one another.

L:   We gather as members of the family of the earth,

P:   Who long to make peace with the Lord and with one another.

A:   Bring us together in your family, O Lord, that we might find happiness and peace in ours.

*Invocation.* O Christ, who teaches us to think of God as our parent and of the world's inhabitants as our brothers and sisters, we turn our thoughts to our kindred. As we celebrate the home, help us to judge it by the high purpose for which it was fashioned, not by the low estate into which it has fallen. Enable us so to renew our ties with the members of our families that our homes will reflect the unity that binds us together in the family of God.

### *Litany*

L:   O God, who gives us life in our families, that we might come together in yours,

P:   Grant that the ties which bind us to one another might bind us ever closer to you.

L:   Let us remember Abraham and Sarah, who despite the rigors of life in a strange land, blessed all the families of earth.

P:   We thank you, dear Lord, for the faith and courage with which they answered your call.

L:   Let us remember Isaiah, who despite the exile that tore families apart, proclaimed a covenant that would unite them again.

P:   We thank you, dear Lord, for the hope and vision with which he inspired your people.

L: Let us remember Jesus of Nazareth, who despite a deep regard for his kin, defined your family on the basis of grace.

P: We thank you, dear Lord, for the strength and joy with which he embodied your love.

L: O God, who gives us life in your family, that we might come together in ours,

P: Grant that the ties which bind us close to you might bind us ever closer to one another.

*Prayer for One Voice.* O God, who has joined all people of all generations as brothers and sisters in a common family, you are our heavenly Parent, and for this we are glad. We adore you because you first adored us; we love you because you first loved us; we seek you because you first sought us. We draw near to you now in behalf of our earthly families because, through the ages, you have drawn near to us in behalf of your heavenly family.

We remember with special gratitude all who, by their love, have taught us the meaning of your love; who, by putting others first, have taught us the meaning of membership in your family. At their best, they have been not only good *to* us, but good *for* us.

The faces of some of these dear ones we now see only in our memories. Yet they still speak to us—reminding us of truths we too seldom pursue, of values we too often compromise, of people we too rarely befriend, of a heritage we too casually abandon. Help us, dear Lord, to honor these shapers of our conscience by listening for your word in their teachings. Let us hear that all humanity has become heir to your promise to the family of Abraham and Sarah; that righteousness is the foundation of your family; that membership in your family dispels anxiety for things and indifference to persons. In these teachings we can seek and find clues to your will. Let us drink from the fountain of their wisdom, that its healing waters might renew our families as it renewed theirs.

We confess, O God, that our generation is late in making this petition. We have become more adept at homebreaking than at homemaking, at tearing families apart than at holding them together, at denying family responsibilities than at meeting them. So now our families are ill-prepared for the pressures that assault them. Too soon children must wrestle with the temptations of adolescence; adolescents, with the burdens of adulthood; adults, with the suspicion that human frailty has become too much for the human family.

We have made the family a battleground, O Lord. The fate and the future of the home hang in the balance, and we are sorely afraid—afraid for ourselves, afraid for our families, and afraid, above all, for the humanity of human beings.

So we pray, dear Lord, for the home. Grant us the will and the wisdom to make it a center for humanizing human beings. If we be children, let us use our power to affect the life of our parents—to bless and not to curse. If brothers and sisters, let us use our power to influence the life of our siblings—to lead and not to mislead. If parents, let us use our power to shape the life of our children—for good and not for evil.

O God, let us remember that if we would take your kingdom seriously, we cannot take our homes lightly. Let us never forget that all the big happenings in our lives have their beginnings in the little happenings in our families.

*Benediction.* O God, who makes us beneficiaries of the families from which we come, make us benefactors of the families to which we belong. If they who went before us did ill, let us learn from the errors of their way. If they did well, let us perfect the good work begun in them. Let our families harvest the fruit of both our good judgment and our good work.

## *Peace with Justice Sunday/World Communion Sunday/Christian Unity*

*Lections:* I Chronicles 16:23-34; Psalm 33; Acts 2:37-47; Matthew 8:5-13

*Call to Worship*
L: Sing a new song unto the Lord—
P: For the Lord has chanted the world into being!
L: The lips of the Lord parted in song,
P: And there was the earth; and there were the heavens.

L:  The breath of the Lord broke forth into song,
P:  And there was the land; and there were the seas.
L:  The voice of the Lord lifted in song,
P:  And there was the one; and there were the two.
L:  O sing a new song unto the Lord—
A:  For the Lord is chanting our world into being!

*Invocation.* Seeing your wounds, O Christ, we are cut to the heart. *Still* they flow; *still* your body bleeds—with every blow to one of your creatures, with every threat to your creation, you are crucified again.

How faithless we are, serving rulers other than you, seeking kingdoms other than yours! How fickle we are, breaking bread in your memory, then brandishing swords in your name![251]

O Christ, we have betrayed you; and by betraying you, we have betrayed one another. The shepherd has been struck; the sheep have scattered.[252] Rise up, O Lord; forgive us, that we might become one, and in the strength of our unity, deny you no more.

*Litany*

L:  That they who rule might seek the welfare of those who serve: This is my desire.
P:  Say the word, Lord, and it shall be so. Blessed are the merciful, for they shall obtain mercy.
L:  That they who have plenty might meet the need of those who have little: This is my desire.
P:  Say the word, Lord, and it shall be so. Blessed are the meek, for they shall inherit the earth.
L:  That they who are many might uphold the rights of those who are few: This is my desire.
P:  Say the word, Lord, and it shall be so. Blessed are those who hunger for justice, for they shall be satisfied.
L:  That they who quarrel might hear the cries of those who long for peace: This is my desire.
P:  Say the word, Lord, and it shall be so. Blessed are the peacemakers, for they shall be called your children.[253]

---

251 See Mark 14:47.
252 See Mark 14:27.
253 Responses inspired by Matthew 5:3-10.

L: Then do not cry, "Peace! Peace!" while battles still rage![254]
P: We have heard your word; we will make it so.
L: Do not shout, "Free at last!" while chains still rattle!
P: We have heard your word; we will make it so.
L: Do not sing, "A land of plenty!" while bellies groan!
P: We have heard your word; we will make it so.
L: Do not say, "Lord, Lord!" while idols still stand![255]
A: We have heard your word; we will make it so!

*Prayer for One Voice.* O God of Sinai, who dispatches prophets from the mountaintops to dash our golden calves to the ground,[256] great are you, and greatly to be praised! In you the world stands firm. It is by *our* hand that the earth trembles. Our hands have forged an assembly of idols, and we have called each of them *Lord.* Why should we marvel that the world shakes when you topple them from their altars?

Why should we wonder that we are not saved by the size of our armies, that we are not delivered by the might of our weapons? Why should we be amazed that we are not redeemed by the scope of our knowledge, or the strength of our convictions, or the glory of our laws? Why should we be astonished that we are not liberated by the charity of a dollar, that we are not freed by the flying of a flag?

O Lord, we are so unlike the centurion! Rare are the times we recognize our weakness and acknowledge your authority over all. Rare are the times we seek great power not for ourselves, but for the sake of another.

Behold your children, Lord! Hear our weeping, our gnashing of teeth! The gods we have fashioned cannot stand; strong they may be, but they are formed from the dust of the earth. They cannot save us: Our armies march, yet peace does not prevail; our weapons restrain, yet security is not achieved; our knowledge increases, yet wisdom does not follow; our convictions speak, yet compassion finds no voice; our laws are writ-

---

254 See Jeremiah 6:14.

255 Inspired by Matthew 7:21-23.

256 Inspired by Exodus 32.

ten, yet justice does not rule; our hopes are pinned on the value of a dollar, on the promise of a flag, yet freedom is not gained.

O God, we have wandered far from you, but your promise reaches even to us! Send the gift of your spirit! We break the bread: Break our gods! We lift the cup: Lift up our faith! We proclaim the word: Proclaim our release!

Release us, Lord, that we might bind ourselves to the spirit and the toil and the triumph of your kingdom! Release us, that we might welcome your peace, receive your wisdom, impart your compassion, establish your justice! We who have aspired to be centurions now declare, "Release us from our will to command, that we might learn to obey your will! Release us, and we will kneel and plead for the healing of those we called servants!"

*Benediction.* As you have spoken, Lord, let it be! Through Christ, your word has been uttered; now, through us, let it be done!

## *Memorial Day/All Saints Day*

*Lections:* Daniel 7:1-3, 15-18; Psalm 149; Ephesians 1:11-23; Luke 6:20-36

### *Call to Worship*

L: Let us praise the God of our ancestors,

P: Who robs death of its sting and the grave of its victory.[257]

L: Let us praise the God of our ancestors,

P: Who fills life with its joy and the future with its hope.

A: O come, let us worship the Lord our God, the same yester-day, today, and forever!

*Invocation.* Gracious God, who weakens the proud and strengthens the meek, awaken us to the glory of faithful obedience to you and humble service to humanity. As we search our heritage for traces of your revelation, grant us clarity of vision, lest we find it where it is absent and deny it where it is present. Let us resolve not only to claim your revelation as our

257 Inspired by I Corinthians 15:55-58.

legacy from your people, but to refine it as our legacy to your people.

*Litany*

L: O God, whose grace through our ancestors has made us hopeless debtors,

P: As we sing our praises to you, help us to remember our debt to them.

L: They forsook the rewards of the mighty for your promise of blessing to the lowly.

P: Help us, O Lord, to walk in their steps.

L: They scorned the comforts of the wealthy for your gift of fellowship with the poor.

P: Help us, O Lord, to walk in their steps.

L: They discounted the opinions of their neighbors for your revelation of truth in their hearts.

P: Help us, O Lord, to walk in their steps.

L: They discarded the laws of retribution for your call to forgiveness of sinners.

A: O Lord, we thank you for the trail of faithfulness blazed by our ancestors. Help us to walk in their steps.

*Prayer for One Voice.* O God, our source of meaning in life and our hope of victory in death, we bow in gratitude for the ties with which you bind us to those who have gone before us. We are especially grateful for the assurance that the end of their journey with us does not spell the end of their journey with you; that their service to you is not limited to the time of their earthly pilgrimage; that their influence on us is not buried with them; that, in ways they never would have guessed and we never could have planned, they continue to guide us, helping us resist the temptation to do evil and quickening our will to do good. Just as we are strangely and wonderfully made in their image, we are strangely and wonderfully linked to them across the generations, and for this, dear Lord, we thank you.

We thank you, in particular, for those departed friends and relatives from whom we learned the fine art and solemn duty of putting first things first: They taught us that, just as we cannot truly worship you without serving humanity, we cannot truly serve humanity without worshiping you; that, just as you love us without regard for our merit or condition, we are to love others without regard for *their* merit or condition; that, just as you could not become one with us without taking risks, we cannot become one with you without taking risks. Help us, dear Lord, to be vulnerable to you, so that, in our hour of trial, we might, with gladness, take risks for your sake and for the gospel's.

We have squandered many risk-taking opportunities, to the peril of our legacy and the discredit of our heritage. We have been quick to claim Christ's company but slow to follow his example. We were told that in your realm the hungry shall be satisfied, the weeping consoled, and the outcast welcomed, but we have not done unto the hungry and weeping and outcast as we would have them do unto us. Instead of adopting the policy of the saints, we have embraced the practice of the sinners—blessing only those who bless us, giving only to those who give to us.

O God, we do not ask you to hide your face from our sin. But we do ask you to break sin's hold upon our lives. As trustees of the spiritual capital of our ancestors, let us become its faithful investors, that we might enrich the heritage we bequeath to our descendants.

O Lord, hear our prayer. We pray in the memory of the dead, who have taught us what you do for us and what you expect from us. We pray also for the sake of the living, whom you would have us teach what you do for them and what you expect from them. As our ancestors served you by instructing us in your will and ways, help us, O Lord, to go and do likewise.

*Benediction.* As with gratitude we celebrate the memory of the faithful dead, let us extend their noble legacy and your righteous rule—by lending to those who do not lend to us, by helping those who do not help us, and by loving those who do not love us.

## Homecoming Sunday

*Lections:* Genesis 28:10-17; Psalm 84; I Peter 2:1-6, 9-10; Luke 15:11-32

### Call to Worship

L:  This is the dwelling place of our God; let us rejoice and be glad in it!

P:  The Lord is the source of all life; let us seek the Lord with all our heart!

L:  The Lord is the giver of all life; let us receive the Lord with all our soul!

P:  The Lord is the goal of all our striving; let us worship the Lord with all our being!

A:  As God has blessed us in our dwelling place, let us bless God in the dwelling place of the Lord!

*Invocation.* O God of those who have gone before us, our hearts swell with gratitude as we enter this sanctuary. While our lives may carry us far away, our memories keep us forever close. Here we were baptized into the household of your people. Here we were introduced to the values we still hope to achieve. Here we first promised to love you with all our heart and mind and soul and strength. Here we first pledged to love our neighbor as ourselves.

O God of those who shall come after us, renew our commitment to your sanctuary, that their memories of this place might enrich their lives for as long as they shall live.

### Litany

L:  O Lord, we come together in your dwelling place, in memory of days gone by.

P:  The building and the faces may have changed, but their influence continues to shape our lives.

L:  Here we were baptized into the community of believers, the body of our Lord.

P:  With gratitude we recall the warmth of that welcome and the strength of that challenge.

L: Here we were taught always to press on toward the goal of your upward call in Christ.[258]

P: With gratitude we recall the depth of that lesson and the diligence of our teachers.

L: Here we were forgiven when we stumbled and given the will to rise again.

P: With gratitude we recall the pain of our separation and the joy of our reunion.

L: Here we were sent forth on our own and assured that we would never journey alone.

P: With gratitude we recall the power of that promise and the grace of its fulfillment.

L: O Lord, we come together in your dwelling place to renew our friendship with your people and our faith in you.

P: May your dwelling place always be a home for others, as this place has been for us.

*Prayer for One Voice.* O God, you have been our dwelling place in all times and places. But here—in this church where we first came to know and love you—you are present to us as nowhere else. We thank you that, just as you have been with us wherever we have gone, you are with us now as we return. You have blessed our home-leaving; bless now our homecoming.

O God, in whose name and for whose reign our ancestors built this church, we praise you for its faithful witness and fruitful service: for the souls it has inspired with its good news of your love; for the minds it has stretched with its reminder of your concern for all creation; for the wills it has strengthened with its insistence on your hard demands; for the hearts it has warmed with its welcome of all your people.

With special gratitude we celebrate those whose trust in your grace and whose obedience to your word gave us a head start in life. Some had few material goods, but they abounded in spiritual treasure. We do not remember them for what they had; we remember them for who they were. We remember that when we needed them most, they were there, and for this, O Lord, we give thanks to them and to you.

---

258 See Philippians 3:14.

We wish we had followed more closely their teaching and example. But we have done what they warned us not to do, and we have failed to do what they urged us to do. We have left untried what they encouraged us to try. We were challenged to make the harmonious family a pattern for our life in the church and in the world. While we may recognize you as our heavenly Parent, we are reluctant to recognize others as our brothers and sisters. The walls that divide the nations are falling faster than the walls that divide our souls. Forgive us, O God, for the dullness of our minds, the hardness of our hearts, the tameness of our spirits. Receive our lamentation over yesterday's failures! And move us from repentance to the faith that seizes today's opportunities and the hope that anticipates tomorrow's blessings. Kindle in us the courage that ignited the hearts of our forebears, that we might dare as they dared to try whatever it is time to try.

Dear Lord, hold up to us your mirror, until we replace the smirk of the elder brother with the smile of the glad father. Send us forth to greet your people as our sisters and brothers, as members of your family and ours. Make us worthy of the heritage of this church, and this church worthy of the heritage of Christ.

*Benediction.* Gracious God, today, as in days past, you have blessed us with your presence in this place. Now, as we leave this place, go with us, that our fond dreams might become precious memories, and our precious memories beget fond dreams.

## A National Observance

*Lections:* Exodus 19:1-9; Psalm 146; Acts 17:22-28; Matthew 25:31-46

*Call to Worship*
L: The eagle is stirring in her nest;
P: Fluttering over her young, she catches them up;
L: She bears them up to lofty places,
P: Even unto the holy mountain.

L: Let me carry you on my outstretched wings and soar into the heavens!
P: Lift up our eyes unto the clouds, and teach your fledglings to fly!
A: By your wisdom let us mount the wind and build our nest on high; by your love let us rise and learn to touch the sky![259]

*Invocation.* We are refugees, Lord. Long we have wandered in the wilderness, slaves who fled from the land of their toil.

Now you have brought us to your holy mountain. Here your voice shall thunder; your word shall strike through the dark of night. Here we will become a holy nation—not because we are mighty, for we are weak; not because we are humble, for we are proud; not because we are wise, for we are foolish—but because you love us,[260] a people you have made one with all other peoples of the earth.

You have broken our shackles, Lord; each hand that has been freed is yours to use. Speak to us, Lord; each word that is spoken shall be ours to heed.

*Litany*
L: I became flesh and dwelled in your midst, full of grace and truth.[261]
P: Surely we beheld you—the servant of the Lord!
L: I staggered among you, demanding bread; I fainted among you, pleading for water—
P: Did we not provide?
L: I was a stranger among you, wanting for care; I wandered among you, clothed in rags—
P: Did we not provide?
L: I was wasted with disease, looking for healing; I cowered in my cell, begging for mercy—
P: Did we not provide?
L: I had no comeliness that you should look at me, no beauty you would admire.

---

259 Inspired by Deuteronomy 32:11-13; Job 39:27-28.
260 See Deuteronomy 7:7.
261 See John 1:14.

P: But surely we recognized you—the servant of the Lord!

L: I was despised, bruised, and rejected; a friend of sorrow, acquainted with grief.

P: But surely we received you—the servant of the Lord!

L: I was the one from whom you hid your face and turned away your eyes. I gave you my back, and you burdened me; I turned my cheek, and you struck me.

P: So we cut you off from the land of the living; we dug your grave among the forgotten.

L: But my purpose shall triumph over yours! I shall rise over you and shake the nations; your rulers shall shut their mouths in awe—

A: For what we had not seen before, we shall now perceive; what we would not hear before, we shall now understand.[262]

*Prayer for One Voice.* O God, in whom we live and move and have our being, we marvel that you have claimed us as your possession, until we remember that all the universe is yours. We boast that you have chosen us as your people, until we recognize that all peoples are begotten by you. We have no cause for pride; only praise. Therefore we sing to you, and bless your name; we declare your glory among the nations, your marvelous works among all the peoples![263]

You, the great unknown, have made yourself known to us. You have revealed yourself as the strong right arm that smashes the chains of slaves and sets upon them the yoke of freedom. You have manifested yourself as the stable-born child who threatens the reign of monarchs and overturns thrones by the rule of love. You have shown yourself as the rushing wind that inspires the hearts of prophets and carries to earth the age of the Spirit. You do, indeed, make yourself known to us; and, in knowing you, we begin to know our world as it could be.

Knowing you, Lord, we no longer can be satisfied with our world as it is. We are your people. You have called us to turn the world upside down by our love,[264] as you overturned the

---

262 Litany is drawn from the Servant Songs of Isaiah 50, 53.
263 See Psalm 96:2-3.
264 See Acts 17:6.

schemes of Pharaoh, the plots of Herod, the intrigues of Caesar. You have dared us to trust—not the mortals who rule over us, whose plans perish with their final breath, but you, who keep faith with us forever. You have made us emissaries of hope, and have sent us to execute justice for the oppressed, to give food to the hungry, to set the imprisoned at liberty, to open the eyes of the blind, to lift up those who are bowed down, to watch over the forsaken and those far from home. You have sent us to all those who are so easily exploited, ignored, or forgotten; to all those whom we so often have regarded as the goats, while we numbered ourselves among the sheep.

Let us not profess to know you, O God, and then deny you by our deeds.[265] Let us not cry, "Lord, Lord!" and then put our will in place of yours. For we who hear your word and do not heed it shall build a house without a foundation, and when the flood rises and rages against it, at once the house shall fall, and its ruin shall be great.[266]

Help us instead to dig deep, to lay our foundation upon the rock.[267] Let us build only on you, and we shall build a world whose peoples, being possessed by you, do not look to rebel; who, being chosen by you, do not seek to flee. Help us to dig deep, and we will find the law you have written on our hearts. You shall be our God, and we will be your people. No longer shall any of us teach our neighbor, saying, "Know the Lord"— all shall know you for themselves, from the least to the greatest.[268]

*Benediction*
L:  Behold, the Lord our God is as close as breath;
P:  The Lord our God is as near as life.
L:  Listen for the voice; receive the word. For this is the pledge we have taken:
P:  All that the Lord asks, we will do.
L:  This is the vow we have spoken:
P:  The will of the Lord shall become our own.

---

265 See Titus 1:16.
266 Inspired by Luke 6:46-49.
267 Inspired by Luke 6:46-49.
268 Drawn from Jeremiah 31:33-34.

L:  And what is this word? What is this will?
P:  That we love the world as we have first been loved.[269]

## Labor Day

*Lections:* Deuteronomy 24:19-22; Psalm 8; I Peter 4:7-11; Mark 10:35-45

*Call to Worship*
L:  Rejoice!
P:  The beginning of all things is at hand!
L:  The cup overflows;
P:  Its power descends from the heavens, and the hand that pours it is the Lord's!
A:  O Lord, our Lord, how majestic is your name in all the earth!
L:  The baptism burns;
P:  Its fire rains down from the sun, and the hand that hurls it is the Lord's!
A:  O Lord, our Lord, how majestic is your name in all the earth!

*Invocation.* O God, you give birth to the cosmos while angels attend, calming the cry of the newborn with a lilting lullaby until it falls asleep on a pillow of clouds.

Your labor, O Lord, endows with dignity *our* labor. In you the void becomes a womb; emptiness becomes the nest of life. In you our striving begets dreams and expectations; our toil spawns skill and determination.

O One who made the moon and stars to be our playmates and the sun to be our life's companion, bless the work of our hands and of our minds. Make them extensions of yours, that we might extend your realm on earth, as it is in heaven.

*Litany*
L:  Once you were slaves in a foreign land. Far from home, your families were broken, shattered like your dreams.

---

269 Inspired by Deuteronomy 10:19.

P: But the Lord heard our cries and led us to freedom. Then every orphan found the way home; every soul, the way to hope.

A: So let us build a quiet place, where none shall be strangers and all shall be friends—we who toiled under a tyrant's hand.

L: Once you were slaves in a foreign land. Far from home, your stomachs were empty, swollen with your anger.

P: But the Lord heard our cries and led us to freedom. Then every mouth was satisfied; every fury, put to rest.

A: So let us make a pleasant planting, of which all the fields and vines shall be shared—we who hungered under a tyrant's hand.

L: Once you were slaves in a foreign land. Far from home, your clothes were tattered, ripped at the seams like tender hearts.

P: But the Lord heard our cries and led us to freedom. Then every garment was the raiment of glory; every heart, the veil of God.

A: So let us weave a robe of all colors,[270] that all the children of God shall wear—we who shivered under a tyrant's hand.

L: Once you were slaves in a foreign land. May the Lord, who heard your prayers in exile and guided your feet to the promised land, hear and guide you from this day—

P: That all our work might twice be blessed:

A: From God to us; from us to others!

*Prayer for One Voice.* O God, your hands mold the earth from clay; your breath forms the clouds of the heavens. You speak, and the warmth of your voice becomes the light of day; you fall silent, and the fullness of your presence becomes the cool of night. You cry for joy, and the oceans swell; you walk upon the waters, and islands grow beneath your feet. You glance at the sky, and a gleam from your eye becomes the sun; the moon and stars soar from a wink and some twinkles. You roll rocks

---

270 Inspired by Genesis 37:3.

from the top of a hill, and they become deer, running races through the fields; you skip stones across the sea, and they become dolphins, playing tag with the waves; you blow flower petals from the palm of your hand, and they become butterflies, skipping rope on the breeze.

What a labor of love is your world, O God! And, so that love's labor should not be lost, you create us, male and female, to tend it.[271]

Who are we that you are so mindful of us, that you make us little less than yourself, crowned with glory and honor? Who are we that you give us dominion over the works of your hands?

Who we are now, Lord, is so much less than we *could* be. You sent Christ to show us that the greatest are those who serve, that the first are those who are last, that the most faithful are those who do what you ask. Yet, like James and John, we would rather ask what you can do for us than what we can do for you. Like James and John, we are more interested in being enthroned as rulers than in acting as stewards. Like James and John, we are more concerned with being served than with being servants.

On the table stands a cup, the chalice of Christ, and you ask, "Are you able to drink?" We cannot, Lord, except by the grace of the gifts you give. Above our heads dances a flame, the fire of the Spirit, and you ask, "Are you able to be baptized?" We cannot, Lord, except by the grace of the gifts you give.

But the gifts we receive are not for ourselves alone. Who are we that you are mindful of us, if we be unmindful of our neighbor? For every human, every butterfly, dolphin, and deer; every star that shines by night and sun that shines by day; every sea and shore; every night and day, every corner of heaven and clod of earth—this is the charge you give us: to protect by *our* works the work you are doing and have done since time began—to glorify with our praise your majestic name!

O Lord, make us able!

---

271 Inspired by Genesis 1.

*Benediction.* The end of all things is now! The beginning of all things is here! Let us rededicate ourselves to the work of creation. Upheld by the power of God, let us hold unfailing our love for one another, that love might understand what our minds cannot grasp and accomplish what our hands cannot do.

## Thanksgiving

*Lections:* Deuteronomy 26:1-11; Psalm 100; Philippians 4:4-9; John 6:25-35

*Call to Worship*
L:  This is the season to remember and to give thanks:
P:  To remember that we do not create the earth from which we reap,
L:  And to give thanks to God for calling us to till the soil;
P:  To remember that others share the toil that brings forth the harvest,
L:  And to give thanks to God for calling us to love and serve our neighbors.
A:  Bless us, dear Lord, as we come together to praise your name and to offer thanks.

*Invocation.* O Lord God, who creates us in your image and makes us stewards of the good earth, we marvel at the trust you place in us. Despite the depths to which we sometimes descend, we know that we are meant for the heights. Despite our crucifixion of the earth, we know that it is made for resurrection. Be with us, O Lord; help us to reclaim the image in which you make us and to renew the earth on which you place us.

*Litany*
L:  O Lord, we gather together to thank you for the good earth,
P:  And for all whose labor turns its fruit into abundant life:
L:  For parents more interested in the character of their children than in the measure of their success;

207

P:  For teachers more attentive to the future of their students than to the fate of their careers;

L:  For farmers more anxious about the quality of their produce than about the quantity of their property;

P:  For doctors and nurses more determined to dispense public health than to accumulate personal wealth;

L:  For lawyers more zealous to guarantee rights than to seek vengeance;

P:  For factory workers more concerned with superior products than with increased production;

L:  For Christians more committed to the empowerment of others than to the elevation of self.

P:  O Lord, we thank you for all the earthly agents of your heavenly will—

L:  For what they do for you, and for what you, through them, do for us—

P:  To bring near the abundant life and enable us to reap the rewards of heaven on earth.

*Prayer for One Voice.* Almighty God, who orders the seasons and charts the flight of the planets, we marvel at the majesty of your creation. We glimpse behind your works a power so removed from us in space and time that we doubt the gap between us can ever be bridged. Yet that gap *was* bridged; you are the one who bridged it—and still bridges it today. In Jesus Christ you revealed your love and beauty and integrity; through the Holy Spirit you continue to bless us with this revelation. No matter where we look, you are there; your spirit is always present: to enlighten us when we are confused; to comfort us when we are troubled; to challenge us when we are complacent; to strengthen us when we are weak; to reassure us when we are afraid; to befriend us when we are lonely; to lead us when we are lost. Long before we begin to seek you, you have already found us. O gracious Lord and Holy Lover, we thank you for the love through which you make your presence known, and we pray for the grace to extend your presence through our love.

We cannot voice this petition without remembering the times we so obscured your presence as to make you appear absent: when we denied the bread of life from heaven by hoarding the loaf of bread from earth; when the deeds of our lives mocked the praise of our lips, substituting the false for the true, the impure for the pure, the unlovely for the lovely, and the mediocre for the excellent.

For all such times, we are deeply sorry. Enable us to erase them from our memory, even as you, O Lord, have blotted them from yours. Set our minds on what is true and pure and lovely and excellent, until with our minds we think your thoughts, and with our hands we work your will.

Many of the good things of life—food and freedom, faith and fellowship, security and serenity, health and hope, peace and prosperity—have come to some of us in great abundance. But more members of the human family live in the grip of poverty than recline in the lap of luxury. If we are among the lucky third of the earth's inhabitants, let us not forget the neglected two-thirds. Help us to remember that, just as these deprived children are your children, they are likewise our brothers and sisters; that, just as you esteem them as members of your family, you expect us to treat them as members of our family. Enable us to assure them, as Jesus Christ assured us, that neither poverty nor ignorance, neither hunger nor thirst, neither nakedness nor sickness, neither class nor culture, neither race nor religion, nor anything in all creation, can ever separate them from your love or from ours. Grant us the grace, O Lord, to express our love for them in costly deed and virtuous life, that our words of thanksgiving might bring forth works of thanksgiving.

*Benediction*

L: O Lord, as you bless our fields with the harvest,
P: Now fill our hearts with generous care;
L: That, as we remember what you do for us in the yield of our lands,
P: We will ponder what we can do for you through the labor of our hands.

## Student Day

*Lections:* Nehemiah 8:1-8; Psalm 1; Romans 12:3-13; Luke 22:24-27

*Call to Worship*

L: Happy are they who walk no more in exile,

P: Who seek no more the way of the fickle, who follow no more the folly of the faint.

L: Happy are they who delight in the Lord,

P: Who lift up their hearts and worship their God, who lift up their hands and shout, "Amen!"

*Invocation.* O Teacher of all truths, we gather before you as one body. With one heart we plead with you to reveal your presence. With one soul we wait for you to proclaim your word. With one mind we reach to you to discover your will. With one strength we rise with you to do your bidding.

O Guide through all mysteries, initiate us into the way that is your way, the truth that is your truth, and the life that is your life. Open the book, and we shall read. Open our ears, and we shall understand.[272]

*Litany*

L: Happy are they who, like the tree that learns to bend, yield before the wind:

W: They do not regard themselves more highly than they should,

M: But outdo one another in showing honor,

A: And, in honoring a sister, honor themselves.

L: Happy are they who, like the vine that reaches its season, yield good and pleasant fruit:

W: They do not rejoice while a brother suffers,[273]

M: But outdo one another in showering mercy,

A: And, in being merciful, find mercy for themselves.

L: Happy are they who, like the stream that runs its course, yield not to temptation:

---

272 Inspired by Mark 12:29; John 14:6.

273 Inspired by I Corinthians 12:26.

210

W:  Therefore, let the prophet who prophesies proclaim the
    Lord's word;

M:  Let the servant who serves do the Lord's will;

A:  Let the teacher who teaches prepare the Lord's people; let
    the student who studies seek the Lord's way!

*Prayer for One Voice.* O God, who exalts the humble and honors
the least, how much we are concerned with our own greatness,
and how little we understand yours! We who measure success
by degrees, what do we know of your grace, which has no
gauge? We who weigh charity on the scales, what do we know
of your mercy, whose burden is light? We who regard prosperity as the reward for faithfulness, what do we know of your
love, which suffers the scandal of a cross?

Blessed are they who delight in your law; who, like trees
planted by streams of water, yield good fruit, and prosper.
"Blessed," you name the righteous. Yet, while we are preoccupied with the dispute over our own greatness, your righteous
ones prepare to die. We hear Christ saying, "Let these words
sink into your ears; I am to be delivered into human hands."[274]
An ominous warning—but either we cannot comprehend or
we lack the courage to comprehend; we can only argue as to
which of us deserves a throne.

Surely, O God, you must weep for the blessed.

We hear Christ saying, "Those who exalt themselves shall
be humbled, and those who humble themselves shall be exalted."[275] A strange prophecy—but either we cannot comprehend or we lack the courage to comprehend; we can only
rebuke the children for wanting to sit upon Christ's knee.

Surely, O God, you must weep for the blessed.

We hear Christ saying, "Go and prepare the passover, that
we may eat. A man carrying a jar of water will meet you; follow
him into the house which he enters, and make ready."[276] An
incredible sign—a man stooping to do a woman's chore—but
either we cannot comprehend or we lack the courage to com-

---

274 See Luke 9:44-45.
275 See Luke 18:14-15.
276 See Luke 22:8ff.

prehend; we can only go on our way, as if this day were like any other.

Surely, O God, you must weep for the blessed.

We hear Christ saying, "This is my body; this is my blood!"[277] A somber word on such a high holy day—but either we cannot comprehend or we lack the courage to comprehend; we can only cast suspicion on those who could be traitors, while we defend our loyalty to the kingdom.

Surely, O God, you must weep for the blessed as Christ wept over Jerusalem. Yet, despite knowing how slowly we learn and how deftly we transform our gifts into grounds for privilege, you promise that we shall never be far from you. We hear Christ saying, "I assign to you a kingdom, that you may eat and drink at my table."[278]

Surely we must weep, O God, for a blessing so undeserved.

O God, we have exalted ourselves; humble us. Turn our concern from our greatness to yours, that we might honor the least of your people. Teach us to receive your grace, which has no gauge; to grant your mercy, whose burden is light; and to embody your love, which suffers even the scandal of a cross.

*Benediction.* O God, teach us to be like the man who pointed the way to the Last Supper by shouldering a woman's jar of water. By bending to bear the burdens of others, we shall learn to stand straight; by being lifted to their feet, others shall learn to fall to their knees.

## Rural Life

*Lections:* Isaiah 28:23-29; Psalm 104:1-23; I Corinthians 3:5-9; Matthew 13:1-9

*Call to Worship*
L:  We gather together to thank our God,
P:  For the life of the soil and the life of the soul.
L:  We gather together to seek God's blessing,
P:  For the fruit of the field and the fruit of the faith.

---

277 See Luke 22:19-20.
278 See Luke 22:28-30.

L:   O Lord, restore our lives like the thirsty lands,[279]
A:   That the laborers in your vineyard might abound.

*Invocation.* Gracious God, who endows us with abilities that set us apart, and creates us with needs that bring us together, we thank you for our diverse gifts and our common needs. You have blessed us with gifts that differ according to your grace and according to our location in time and place; make us quick to celebrate them, stressing not their uniqueness but their use. And let us boast, if boast we must, not of the gifts we have, not even of the needs we meet, but of you, our Creator and Redeemer.

*Litany*
L:   Bless the Lord, O my soul; the Lord is very great!
P:   How wonderful in counsel is our God; how excellent in wisdom:
L:   Instructing the sun to rise and set,
P:   That we might go to our work in the morning, and see to our labor 'til evening falls!
L:   Teaching our hands to till the soil,
P:   That we might have bread to strengthen our heart and bring forth food to feed the whole earth!
L:   Anointing some of us to plant, and others of us to water,
P:   That the Spirit might breathe life into the seed, as we labor with the Lord!
L:   If the seeds are scorched by the sun, or choked by the thorns—
P:   Let us not doubt that the harvest will be full; what the Lord intends shall not return empty:
L:   The word of the Lord shall yield good fruit—
P:   The pleasant planting shall produce life abundant, and all shall eat and be satisfied!

*Prayer for One Voice.* O Lord our God, Creator of heaven and earth, the wonder of your universe astounds us. When we lift our eyes to the heavens, we are struck by the power with which you move the planets. When we cast our eyes about the earth,

---

279 Inspired by Psalm 26:4.

we are overwhelmed by the wisdom with which you order creation—separating night from day, making one season follow another, dispensing water and light, that we might fulfill your command to be fruitful and multiply.[280] When we turn our eyes inward, we marvel as never before, that you would entrust a heritage so vast and splendid to stewards so weak and fickle. Our reason tells us that your confidence defies explanation. But our faith tells us there *is* an answer, and the answer is your love—the love that, in creation, brings us into being; that, in Christ, reconciles us to you and to one another. For your love, and for your confidence in us, we thank you, dear Lord.

We must admit that we give you ample cause for doubting your own wisdom. Unlike the farmer, who knows that the harvest depends upon the seed, we entertain thoughts and perform deeds as if they will not produce consequences. Unlike the farmer, who knows when to play by the rules and when to play by ear, we do not master the lessons of experience, relying neither on reason when we could, nor on imagination when we should.

O God, grant us the patience and persistence and common sense of the farmer, that we might learn the lessons of experience. As you have taught the farmer the need for innovation, bless us with the gift of imagination and the capacity to change. Deliver us from the temptation to reduce all of life to a set of rules. Let us never forget that you transcend our rules—that we can forsake our rules without forsaking you. You are the living God, the Lord of today as of yesterday!

O Lord, teach all of us to care for one another as you care for us. Today we ask especially that you help us to care for the world's farmers, assuring them that there is nothing small about a job that produces food for the hungry, that increases its yield thirtyfold, sixtyfold, even a hundredfold. We thank you for the life and labor of these care-givers of the earth, laborers worthy of their hire. Be with us, O God, as we grant them not only the reward that is their just due but the dignity that is their human right.

---

280 See Genesis 1:28.

CELEBRATION OF SPECIAL OCCASIONS

*Benediction.* O God, as you have made harvests different from one another to meet our needs, you have made us different from one another to cultivate our gifts. Now send us forth, so to use the fruit of the field that we might multiply the fruit of faith.

## Urban Life

*Lections:* Zechariah 8:1-17; Psalm 46; Revelation 21:1-4, 22-27; Matthew 9:35-38

### Call to Worship

L: O God, from cities built with human hands we turn—
P: We come to the holy city, that we might learn:
L: Show us the truth that will check our lust for gain,
P: The secret that will stop the spread of pain,
L: The love that will end the strife that tears us apart—
A: Until with you and our neighbors we are one in heart!

*Invocation.* O God of the prophets and apostles, who in your name proclaimed judgment on the old Jerusalem only to herald the promise of a new Jerusalem, kindle in us the faith you ignited in them. When we behold in our cities the evils that undid the old Jerusalem, we are perplexed, but not unto despair.[281] Set our minds on the glories of the new Jerusalem; anoint us to bring it from heaven to earth. As we labor to turn our cities into your cities, make us fit, O Lord, for their habitation.

### Litany

L: By the roads leading into our cities, we sit down and weep when we remember Zion,[282]
P: The heavenly city for which we long, a model for the cities in which we live:
L: In Zion the old walk the streets without fear, and the young play in safety—

281 See II Corinthians 4:8.
282 See Psalm 137:1.

P: But here the young are exposed to danger, and the old are hunted down like prey;

L: In Zion the rulers speak the truth in love, and the judges dispense justice with mercy—

P: But here the judges tailor verdicts to status, and the rulers trade truth for gain;

L: In Zion the wealthy wage war against poverty, and the gifted break the chains of ignorance—

P: But here the gifted guard the fortress of knowledge, and the wealthy make peace with indifference.

L: O Lord, let Zion become the workplace of earthly builders, not just the playground of holy dreamers—

P: Lift us up, and lead us back to our cities, that we might lay the foundation of your city on earth!

*Prayer for One Voice.* Eternal God, who creates us for community with one another, we thank you for the ties with which you bind us into one family. Despite the temptation to pursue our destiny independent of one another, you compel us to seek fulfillment in dependence upon one another. We cannot live without bread, yet we cannot put bread on the table without the help of others. We cannot live without order, yet we cannot keep order without the consent of others. We cannot live without friends, yet we cannot make friends without the presence of others.

O Lord, we have come together in cities, that we might satisfy our common needs in mutual dependence. As a consequence, we have unparalleled opportunities, and we face unprecedented dangers. O God, make us equal to the opportunities and alert us to the dangers, that the cities we build might anticipate that city of which you are the builder and maker.[283]

We do not utter this petition lightly. We recall only too well our past failures to pay due heed to danger. Though warned not to withhold education from the poor, we have been more concerned that education be funded locally than that it be distributed fairly. Though warned not to widen the gap be-

---

283 See Hebrews 11:10.

tween the haves and the have-nots, we have been more concerned with personal privilege than with social justice. Though warned not to ignore the diet of the disadvantaged young, we have been more concerned about the responsibility of parents than about the nutrition of children. Though warned not to ignore the connection between health and wealth, we have been more concerned that those receiving medical care pay for it, than that those needing medical care receive it. By tuning out these warnings, we have turned our cities into battlegrounds between the sexes, the classes, and the races. We have sown the wind, and we are reaping the whirlwind.

Now the warnings are more shrill, and the opportunities more limited. Things are as they are because we have done what we should not have done, and have failed to do what we should have done. For these failures, whether of commission or omission, we implore your forgiveness, dear Lord. And we ask for another chance to overcome evil with good: to turn our cities from citadels of crime into centers of culture; from havens of despair into sanctuaries for hope; from strongholds of indifference into dwelling places of compassion; from retreats from personal responsibility into arenas of social obligation.

O God, the cities are full of people—our people and your people. Help us to rediscover our kinship with them and with you, that our cities, like your promised new Jerusalem, might become places where we worship you in truth and beauty, and serve the neighbor in love and duty.

*Benediction.* The cities into which Christ sends us are filled with harassed and helpless people, wandering like sheep without a shepherd.[284] The crowds are vast, but the laborers are few. We pray, O Lord, not only for more laborers, but for laborers who will greet the crowds with the compassion of the Good Shepherd.

---

284 Inspired by Matthew 9:36.

# Index of Scriptural Passages

# INDEX OF SCRIPTURAL PASSAGES

# LITANIES AND OTHER PRAYERS

220

# INDEX OF SCRIPTURAL PASSAGES

# LITANIES AND OTHER PRAYERS

# INDEX OF SCRIPTURAL PASSAGES